MY OTHER BROTHER

Male Spirituality Through The Lens

of Biblical Brothers

Timothy Nicinski

First Edition

To my brothers, all of them
May you always be aware of God's love

TABLE OF CONTENTS

ROMANS 8:29-30 NRSV

For those whom he foreknew he also predestined to be conformed to the image of his Son, in order that he might be first born within a larger family.

And those whom he predestined he also called; and those whom he called he also justified; and those whom he justified he also glorified.

INTRODUCTION

The relationships between brothers run the spectrum from love to loathe, happiness to hatred, reward to resignation. As a brother myself, I have felt all of these emotions at one time or another. The emotions have come in waves that lasted brief moments, or been held over the course of many years. The emotions that I experienced occurred as many times and for as many reasons as there were time frames during childhood. The emotions were as different and as varied as the cycle of the weekends of adolescence, and of the seasons of adulthood. My brothers have been the source of many shared laughs from jokes, smiles as supportive team members, and joy as the result of enthusiastic partners on road trips. We have also been bitter rivals for attention both within and beyond the family unit, argumentative opponents across numerous topics and beliefs, disgruntled co-workers completing chores, and frustrated employees in family businesses. In some instances, my sibling relationships have grown into great friendships that last a lifetime and in other situations, these relationships remain broken and a source of regret. The foundation of this book is to examine our relationships with our brothers. In these pages, I hope that you will find comfort and clarity in examining your relationship. I also hope that this text will provide reflection and guidance as we continue to lead lives as children of God, brothers, and members of the human race.

Our brothers are not ours to choose. In some cases, we choose our friends over family, and the choice of family is the same as walking to the ballot box holding your nose to pull the lever, recognizing that we are voting for something or someone we find offensive. At other times, our brother is the person we would stand by in the darkest hour, the hardest times, the person who refuses to back down from supporting us, regardless of the situation. That is why, when a man announces to another, that "you are like a brother to me" it holds such power and sway in our emotional lives. We welcome this opportunity for closeness and commitment because of our experience of the challenges around being a brother.

However, our biological brothers represent blood of our blood and bone of our bone. We share the closest DNA with these men in the same way that all of society in some way shares the identical DNA. The shared nurtured home experience of adoptive brothers seem to hold this parallel experience, bridging biological gaps inherent to very close friends. When we think that our most profound us is God, we must also accept that our deepest selves, and maybe even more than we may want to admit, is our other brother.

This book is an opportunity for us to reflect on our relationships as brothers. There may be some similarities and situations that cross the dividing line between other siblings, however, that is simply not a history that I can speak from or write from with the knowledge and authority I find in being a brother. This book is inspired by both my relationships and the stories I have been honored to hear about from other men and their relationships as brothers. I hope that through our time together we can come to terms in our relationship with God and our brothers for a richer and fuller life.

Whatever the relationship, our brothers are a part of us, and some of our greatest jealousies and rivalries come from them. In historic texts, the eldest brother is expected to be the leader of the family. The eldest receives the largest share, if not the entire estate, of the father's farm and generally reflects the biggest, strongest, and best prepared of the clan. The remaining siblings fall into the category of "also rans" and insignificant footnotes of the family lineage and dynasty. Our brothers are our first adversaries and partners, nemeses and allies. Regardless of the present state of our sibling relationships, in our siblings, we feel our closest loves and bonds. I believe that to be complete, we must embrace the entire realm that these other brothers represent. And admit, we too represent someone else's "other brother." We each fall along the ordinal pecking order of the family and in so doing are interdependent with our siblings. Being the "Other" is not to be cast off from the family dynamic or comradery between brothers, but to be unique, special, and outside the orbit of our siblings. Originally, the other brother was anyone younger than the eldest, however in the present configuration we may all hold the title of "other brother." Now, to be the "other brother" is simply to be a sibling.

When we stop to hear the small voice within ourselves, the authentic voice of God, we must consider that He speaks to both our brother and us. The characteristics that we most love and dislike about our brothers are commonly the characteristics we most love and dislike about ourselves. I believe it was Carl Jung who said, "Everything that irritates us about others can lead us to an understanding of ourselves."[1] This does not mean that if we are upset about a sibling that is an abuser, that we are an abuser. That is the symptom. The deep analysis is that in reflecting on a behavior, we are aware of the challenges we have with anger and emotional outbursts that remain unchecked. The frustration that we experience as witnesses to these actions may be mined to uncover similar measures found in our reaction to stimuli. In the late eighties and early nineties, it seemed that the therapists said that we were more and more like our parents and that the challenges we faced in changing our own identity required us to change our behavior and become independent from our parents. We so often said that we did not want to grow up and be like our parents or say the things our parents said only to find ourselves repeating their scripts word for word. In this same way, the rivalry and ambition that we trademark with our siblings is also a part of that same neurological makeup. This kind of thinking is supported by psychologist Daniel

---

[1] *Patrick Hessman, Thought Catalog, Why it's important to understand that we hate others for what we hate about ourselves, March 7, 2017.*

Shaw of the University of Pittsburgh when he describes the closeness that siblings share that we do not even share with our parents. Shaw explains in *Time* magazine: "In general, parents serve as the big picture role as doctors on grand rounds. Siblings are like nurses on the ward. They are there every day."[2] Our brothers shared the same house at times as well as parents, therefore the blueprint of experience is mutual between brothers (and other siblings of course). In essence, when we actively work at being different from our brothers, the result is often the opposite effect. The paradox is, the harder we pull away from our sibling, the more we resemble them.

The Bible is filled with stories of brothers. Some families are represented by two and some are described through many. The tribes of Israel were merely the families of the original sons or brothers from history. The birth order of the people of the Bible at times is as important as the activities that make up their lives. In any case that birth order, or as we call it today, the ordinal position is mentioned, the information plays a part in the story. As small or as vast as it may be, the stories recorded in the Bible provides historical or allegorical insight into the events and outcomes that are crafted by the birth order.

The effects of sibling rivalry are a part of the family dynamic today and were a part of the family dynamic in the Bible as well. The competition was there between Cain and

---

[2] *"Time Magazine," The New Science of Siblings, July 10, 2006. Page 48, Jeffrey Kluger*

Abel as well as Esau and Jacob, and existed right through to the relationship the Apostles had with each other as John and James tried to attain the position of the right and left hand of Jesus in heaven. The existence of sibling conflict runs the gamut in the Bible, from murder and slavery, to pranks and favor. Sibling rivalry has been well documented and is integral to the possible effects of birth order on personality development. Research in the field invites parents to treat siblings in an equal manner to diminish conflict, which is supported by Sulloway when he surmises,"... it may prompt greater emphasis on promotion of positive parenting styles which have been shown to attenuate a great deal of the potentially detrimental effects of sibling rivalry."[3] Sibling rivalry represents only one facet of the many sides of the jewel of brotherhood.

The brothers of the Bible also represented the tightest of bonds, the willingness to support the work of another and ultimately to forsake a life, with and for, blood kin. The Bible provides examples that coincide with the way families develop today. There are nuclear and extended families, blended and single parent families, close knit and disconnected families. In each case, when the book, chapter, or verse includes information about the family, the chances are good that the reference is valuable to the lesson.

Historically, agrarian families were organized based on birthright and blessing. The eldest was given a more

---

[3] *Born to Rebel: Birth Order, Family Dynamics, and Creative Lives, Frank J. Sulloway, Random House, 1996.*

significant share than the youngest. At times, the most inexperienced or younger brothers were forced to leave the family and "make their own way" because the share that was remaining was not enough to sustain a family. The blessing of the father is that of total power and authority of his worldly possessions. The blessing of the father was attached to the cattle, the land, the gold and silver, and eventually the pecking order of responsibility in future generations. The birthright of the first son makes him the family priest, overseer of spiritual and sacred matters for the family. "The eldest son of the family, the first born, received upon his father's death, a spiritual inheritance."[4] He becomes leader of the clan and overall final arbiter of disagreements and the most influential voice of the tribe and the one person who all members of the family must defer to as long as the members of the family stay within the original confines of the family property. The birthright is passed on from one generation to the next, with the responsibility to keep in contact with God. The spiritual leader of the household goes before the Lord to make decisions and carry out the word of God for the family. What is impressive is how rarely God, is recorded in the Bible to connect with the eldest brother to carry out the work of the Lord beyond the family. Instead, God ends up with the son without birthright to be the standard bearer for the covenant work. The eldest son, it

_____

[4] _Jacob and Esau: Birthright and Blessing,_ Rev. Wallace H. Heflin, The McDougal Publishing Company, 1994, p. 11.

seems, is already heavily laden with the things of his earthly father which distract him from the spiritual voice of God to breakthrough for a deeper relationship which allows the second son to be available to carry the load of vocation and the work of his Heavenly Father. The focus of God in this way dictates that we are His children and only come to the world through our parents. God decides the true birthright and the share of the kingdom to be parceled out. While this is not set in stone, the Bible seems to use this dynamic to share the story of humanity's relationship with God. If we consider the "other brother" as the marginalized or poor of the family, then maybe the portion for the other brother supports Father Pedro Arrupe's 1968 letter reminding the world of God's preferential option for the poor. This comment, made by Father Arrupe echoed Matthew 25:40, "whatever you did for the least of these brothers, you did for me."

Today, parents focus on wills and testaments that often provide equal portions amongst the entire family. In retrospect, brother or not, jealousy is a dangerous emotion. However, we are called by God to meaningful relationships with each other and the Lord. As a general rule of thumb, siblings receive equal shares and in some cases, if wealth dictates, shares are provided to cousins and grandchildren. The eldest does not automatically take possession of the family empire (if one even exists). The evening out of family legacies has reduced the value of birth order, and in so doing possibly reduced the temperament needed by younger siblings to cast out on their own and make a way that is a path through a previously uncharted area. The same thinking would result in barricading the temperament and desire to seek a closer relationship with God in these younger siblings. The possibilities are endless to the weakening of bonds with God. The younger sibling does not need to be a seeker. Besides the absence for searching for deeper meaning with God, the new family dynamic may remove the potential for inspired actions on behalf of the younger sibling. The younger sibling does not need to follow a new path for independence since his financial needs are covered (if an inheritance exists) in the present family structure. In the absence of any windfall, which most children live with today, the spiritual component of this journey is absent or remains dormant within the heart. The final analysis as to what significant effect it will have on our world and our spiritual climate is unknown. A possible solution would require humanity to search more fervently for this connection to God and opportunity to make this birthright and blessing connection.

Regardless of ordinal position, I believe that God does call all of us to a loving relationship with the Lord and one another. The authority of birthright and blessing may come from our earthly parents, who select a standard bearer for the tribe. However, God does not seem to follow those cultural norms and instead calls all and provides for the ones who acknowledge that voice and consent to the proposal.

In a similar way that Nicodemus struggled with the teaching of Jesus in reference to seeing the Kingdom of God within being born again, we too must grapple with acquiring the soul of the other brother to accept the birthright and blessing of God. The apparent acceptance of the grace and birthright for us is not predestined by our ordinal position. Instead we must open our hearts to the gifts given by our Father God to accept all the fruits that are granted by Him. You undoubtedly cannot reenter the womb as Nicodemus points out to be born again and you cannot change your birth order and thereby renounce your ordinal position. You may however, humble your soul to God and accept the ordinal position in His family and bask in both the birthright and blessings that He offers you and your life.

The remainder of this work offers a glimpse of men throughout the Bible who have chosen the birthright and blessing of God. In some ways, the characters compare and contrast with a sibling to clarify the gifts, and at other times the separation is also a part of the story. In every case, the characters and settings support a more significant story of God in our lives, up close and personal with real skin and texture.

CHAPTER ONE

Cain And Abel

The story of Cain and Abel is one of disappointment that becomes jealousy, jealousy that festers into anger, and anger that burns red hot to murder. The passive aggressive and then aggressive behavior of Cain nearly destroys the gift of human life so precious to God.

The surprise that Abel may have felt reminds me of a childhood memory of playing basketball on the aged courts in a park in my neighborhood. I vividly remember the pain I felt as I slid across the macadam after being shoved by another kid. I will never forget my surprise in being blocked and fouled the first time playing pick-up basketball on that ragged court that left me extracting gravel out of my bloody forearm. The scrape burned, of course, but the shock burned worse. At some moment, that shooting around activity became a game where one person decided to defend me with a little more aggression than I expected. The game changed that day, and I, unaware of the physical aspect of being denied access to the hoop, had learned too late the meaning of fortified defense.

At first glance, the conflict between Cain and Abel would appear to be a sibling rivalry. The critical component missing is that Abel did not know that he was in any competition. He is not aware that his brother is thirsting for his blood when they go to the field. Abel doesn't know about the conversation between God and Cain. The author of Genesis does not communicate to the reader that Abel knows Cain's countenance has fallen. Abel is unaware that sin knocks on the door of Cain's heart. The silence of the narrative suggests that Abel walks with his brother in fellowship and family unity. Cain slays the trusting Abel out of a context of surprise. Abel is not in rivalry with his brother because he hears the word of the Lord. God's message to love your neighbor as you love yourself is spoken to all those who hear His voice. Abel does not proclaim this truth because he is unaware that not everyone is listening intently to the Lord. The surprise of his brother's anger and assault is a surprise to the reality that anyone exists outside the loving relationship of God.

This may seem naive but the story of Cain and Abel does not provide any precautionary hints to Abel in dealing with Cain. The invitation of Cain to Abel to go out to the field does not have any foreshadowing toward Abel that he should be on guard. The dynamic between the brothers and between humanity and God seemed to be in harmony. The account reminds me of a post dinner walk on a fall afternoon. The brothers, having just celebrated a time of ritual offering, were strolling through the field, as two siblings might walk through their boyhood neighborhood after Thanksgiving dinner, reminiscing with full bellies about the holiday. Abel goes to the field as a brother walks off a good meal with his sibling, without expecting of any surprises or danger. I can't imagine being attacked, being so off guard in that stroll through the neighborhood and I envision Abel would feel the same safety walking through the fields with his brother.

Abel takes this unguarded position of trust without regard for his parents behavior in the Garden of Eden. This behavior tempts us as spiritual seekers, as well as, simply inquisitive readers to wonder if Cain and Abel were aware of their parents' transgressions, the mercy of God, and the entire forward to the neighborhood of existence. If Abel and Cain are aware, then at some level it seems that the lesson of the fall was digested by Abel but remained beyond the understanding of Cain.

The history of the first family of the world is the return from sin to the reconnection with God. Cain was the eldest son of Adam and became a farmer. Abel was the second son or "other brother." He was a shepherd which was not exactly the most reputable career choice in ancient times. Since Adam and Eve were removed from the Garden of Eden, Adam was a farmer and would work the harvest, from the ground. The position of power and direct lineage within the family would naturally pass to Cain. Cain knew this and knew his father's favor. Clearly, Cain would be surprised when his brother Abel's offering to the Lord was more pleasing.

The fact that Abel and Cain are not on the same page spiritually never enters the mind or heart of Abel. Abel does not seem aware of the damaged relationship his parents have with God through their transgressions at the Tree of Knowledge that was forgiven by the Lord and repaired through Yahweh's mercy which restores the first family to the journey of life found within the spiritual framework of a loving Lord after the exit from Eden.

The question that seems logical to ask is why is the sacrifice of Abel is more pleasing? Author and minister Mel L. Piper provides two explanations for the acceptance of Abel's offering over Cain's. Piper describes in his book "Cain and Abel: The Real Story," how the gift from Abel is both a blood sacrifice and a gift of faith. These two reasons, according to Piper, are an example of what is needed and acceptable to God as an offering. Abel provided the first and best sheep of his flock. He also provided the "fat portions." The King James Version translates the same section as "the fat thereof." This portion is later described in both Exodus and Leviticus as part of the sin offering. Abel knows that he needs to provide more than the firstling. He knows this because he is listening for God to give orders. In the same way that Moses will notice the burning bush, Abel is focused on the words of his Holy Father. "Abel was involved in a blood sacrifice. We are told that Abel brought his offering and the fat thereof. As we saw, the animal had to give up its life; it had to pour out its life blood as a sacrifice. God used the blood of animals to cover the sins of mankind."[5]

---

[5] *Cain and Abel: The Real Story*, Mel Piper, Christian Publishing, 1971, pg. 12.

In a text by John Byron, the author provides additional layers of reasoning behind the conflict of what is given to God by the brothers. The interpretation found in the Septuagint (the Greek translation of Hebrew Scripture often noted as LXX) described the language associated with the transaction in this way, "...Cain's sacrifice might indicate an offering that would be divided between the altar and the worshipper. Whereas Abel handed over the entire gift to God, Cain kept some of the sacrifice for himself. This translation of Cain's name, therefore, may further hint at a lack of generosity in Cain, a concern with himself and his possessions possibly representing a defect in his character contrasted with Abel's open handedness."[6] The narrative hints toward Cain holding something back in the offering. However, the "why?" is unclear. Is the reason based on whether he is saving something for a rainy day, protecting his family wealth or simply focused on his own economic status? The answer could also be found in the ordinal position.

The first ordinal position holds great responsibility and it seems that Cain has many important thoughts on his mind as the eldest child. It seems that the concern for the family wealth and position clouds a bit of his decision making when it comes to his relationship with God. Underlying this mindset is his name. If we continue in the line of reasoning associated with the offering, the name "Cain" hints at future expectations. John Byron presents

---

[6] *Cain and Abel in Traditional Text,* John Byron, Brill, Boston, 2011, page 42.

the opinion of Philo the Hellenistic Jewish philosopher about Cain when he writes, "...the crux of Philo's analysis is not whether it is an animal or grain offering. For Philo, his interpretation of Cain is wrapped up in his understanding of Cain's name. Since 'Cain' means 'possession,' Philo consistently portrays Cain as a greedy individual only seeking to gain more...The result of Philo's interpretation is that the responsibility for the rejected offering belonged to Cain. Cain was a greedy worshipper who did not give God all of the offering."[7] I am not sure that Cain is greedy, however it seems that God calls both brothers to a relationship and Abel seems to comply and Cain is either distracted by wealth and possessions that may or may not result in greed or he simply chooses not to interpret the voice of God in the same manner as his brother Abel. In either instance, the voice of anger swells in Cain and he hears a message of murder for his unwitting brother.

The anger and disappointment of Cain were obvious and God spoke to Cain about his reaction and feelings toward Abel. "The Lord said to Cain, Why are you angry, and why has your countenance fallen? If you do well, will you not be accepted? And if you do not do well, sin is lurking at the door; its desire is for you, but you must master it." The warning was simply not enough and Cain persuades his brother into the field and eventually slays him. God punishes Cain for the murder

---

[7] *Cain and Abel in Traditional Text*, John Byron, Brill, Boston, 2011, page 43.

of his brother in two parts. He is separated from his family, and given a mark by which he is protected but cast out from his community and relationship with God. The rejection by his Heavenly Father seemed too profound a consequence to bear in addition to the scolding and the condemnation that marked him with both a protective yet shunning "sign" to the outside world. Therefore, he never returned to any community and remained a wanderer for the rest of his life.

It is important to note, that in the same manner that God forced Adam and Eve from the Garden of Eden, God forces Cain out, yet does not withhold Heavenly love. God could have punished Cain with death, however God chooses leniency and future redemption from a place of love.

So what of Abel? We know little of the second son of Adam and Eve beyond his vocation, his provident choice from God, and his eventual demise. The name Abel has been translated with more than one meaning including "son" and "puff of air." The first translation honors Abel for being so important that the name "son" is all he needs to live as a beloved child. The second translation reflects both his brief existence in scripture but more importantly his freedom from the anxiety and anguish that Cain experiences. Abel's ability to experience the flow of love from God as well as a sense of being chosen, is also an appealing translation that encompasses a spiritual nature. The translation as "puff of air" provides an ethereal calm and spiritual flexibility to his character. Unfortunately, Abel's short life does not reach the conclusion that would clarify which meaning most matched his existence.

The next question is how does God continue His work through this first family? The chosen son is dead and the eldest son, Cain, is sent off from the story. God continues the first family journey with the third son of Adam and Eve. The third son is named Seth. Seth is the patriarch of the lineage that carries the story to Noah through Enosh, Kenan, Mahalalel, Enoch, Methuselah, and Lemach. The name Seth means founder in Hebrew. Seth certainly is the founder. With the separation of Cain and Abel from the Godly path of humankind, Seth is the bedrock of the holy family that reaches Noah. We know that Noah and his sons are found to be the only righteous men on earth when God chooses to flood the world. The Lord begins again His world, this time reinforcing the connection to the simple request laid out in Deuteronomy 5:33 "You must follow exactly the path that the Lord your God has commanded you, so that you may live, and that it may go well with you, and that you may live long in the land that you are to possess." Seth would carry this instruction out before Moses would spell it out to God's chosen people before they entered the Promised Land.

We are fortunate that Seth carries out the purpose given him by God. The name Seth we learn from Calvin Kendell, which means "appointed or resurrection"[8] is indicative of the path he follows. Seth carries the spiritual link and lineage of Abel in listening to the voice of God

---

[8] _On Genesis BEDE,_ Calvin B. Kendall, Liverpool University Press, Glasgow, 2008, page 160.

and holding fast to the call on his life. Kendell continues, "He was 'appointed' for Abel not only in order of birth, but also deservedly, of virtue, filling the place of his brother. His devotion of mind is also shown to have passed to his progeny..."[9] Seth becomes the spiritual laborer in the field that reaps what it is that God guides him to sow. Seth is the journeymen of the story putting the hard work to his back in the day to day holy life. He is not flashy and he does not draw an enormous amount of recorded information in the Bible or from those who log commentary. Seth is a humble trusty that stewards the word of God and the valuable lineage of the family line to Abraham. Seth is able to succeed where his brothers fail. He must have carried incredible baggage based on the history of his parents and the tragedy of his brothers. He recognizes the subtle nuances of what God desires. He is straightforward in his living and loving in his worship. Seth is the salt of the earth.

In chapter five of Genesis, the story of creation and the making of humankind is copied. This replay of the story which then leads to Seth is an example of a renewal of the human experience. As Norman Cohen writes, "Since biblical narratives are so very terse and the sketches of biblical characters so fragmentary, the inclusion of any particular lexical item may be of great significance. Choices of individual words, syntax, narrative structure, the repetition

---

[9] *On Genesis BEDE,* Calvin B. Kendall, Liverpool University Press, Glasgow, 2008, page 160.

of particular motifs as well as selective silence can all be seen as crucial threads in the weaving of a fabric of meaningful exposition. It is precisely because biblical narrative style is so laconic that each and every piece of information can lead to multiple interpretations. As Robert Alter stated, 'the sparsely sketched foreground of the biblical narrative implies a large background, dense with possibilities.'"[10] The results of Seth's success point to the attention that the Genesis author puts on the reboot of the entire human descendent list. Sometimes, the simplest statements are profound, and that is how Ronald Eisenberg captures the essence of Seth. He writes, " According to legend, by killing Abel and incurring the death penalty, Cain would have returned the world to its primordial state of 'tohu va vohu' (complete emptiness). If not for the birth of Seth, the human race would have ceased to exist (Gen. R. 2:3)."[11] The record presented in this manner sets the course for us as brothers to cherish this new opportunity and learn from our past errors. As siblings, we have ringside seats to our brother's success and failure. We can learn through our own failures, or we can take notes from our close proximity to the action. We can ask if we are our brother's keeper or we can state that we are our brother's keeper. If we ask, the lesson of Cain and Abel is lost, but if we pronounce, then we have learned a vital lesson and accept our responsibility for the well-being of our relatives and our siblings through one God.

---

[10] *Two That Are One, Judaism, Norman J. Cohen page 331-332.*
[11] <u>*Essential Figures in the Bible,*</u> *Ronald L. Eisenberg, Aronson, New York, 2013, page 180.*

In the end, we must examine the words of Cain as he responded to God's question "Am I my brother's keeper?" This is an unequivocal yes. Without question, we are our brothers' keepers since, the Bible makes it evident that we are not our brother's murderer. When Abel's action is deemed good and worthy, Cain is given the opportunity to stand with his brother and not only celebrate but support and maybe not duplicate but certainly use that which God has established as good as a framework for behavior and relationship with God. The power of jealousy was incredibly strong for Cain. It was an emotion he could not overcome. In retrospect, brother or not, jealousy is a dangerous emotion. However, we are called by God to meaningful relationships with each other and the Lord. We are not called to be drones or mindless followers of God. Instead, we are welcomed into our relationship with God in a way that honors who we are as unique in our own bodies, minds, and hearts. The story of Cain and Abel gives us a model of relationship beyond our own households, but truly an engagement with all people. The reaction of jealousy and anger takes more from us than we can express. The effort and energy used to exact revenge or outperform another person based on our sense of inadequacy does us great harm. Instead, in the light of witnessing our brother's good gift, we are the people who must stand by their side. We must as the saying goes, "Back our brother's play." In every instance, we are given the opportunity to make the choice of Cain. Will we listen to the Lord and stand by our brother or listen to the lesser gods of greed, jealousy and anger that crowd into our mind and kill our brothers? We do well to celebrate in the success of others. This has a figurative component which I anticipate is coming through clearly in the text. The blood of our brothers may or may not call out to God from the ground however, our sharp words and undercutting actions truly harm them with wounds that may be too great to overcome. We must be honest and righteous in our treatment and duty to them whether they are our flesh and blood or just our Christian spiritual family.

The incarnation tells us that God came in the flesh and was the manifestation of prayer. The prayer had flesh and blood attached. The prayer went into the community and engaged people in a real way. In Christ, people experienced miracles, were healed, and even raised from the dead. By putting on Christ in baptism, we as Christians, are invited to engage with our flesh and bone. As Ronald Rolheiser writes, "When we pray "through Christ" more is involved than merely asking God in Heaven to make some kind of intervention. The community too, and we ourselves, must be involved not just in petition but also in trying to bring about what the petition pleads for."[12] The simple statement that someone or some group is in our thoughts and prayers, is not only theist and unchristian, but removes us from our responsibility as the body of Christ. When we are questioned about events and actions of the day, the words may come from so many sources, but with the core of being, we must know that questions, all questions that

---

[12] *The Holy Longing.* Rolheiser, Ronald. Doubleday 1999. Pg. 84.

prompt us to the treatment of humanity are flowing from God. The response is part of the place we find in the brotherhood of all people. Are we surprised by the evil that is the hearts of others? Are we our brothers' keepers? Or, how may I serve you and your people Lord?

The invitation from God does not come once and pass us forever, but comes to us again and again in small ways and expansive ways. The challenge from God is given each day and not simply on Sunday. The longing of God for us, as we too long for God may be subtle and may be boisterous, but it arrives just the same.

There is an old Hebrew saying: "The seeds of Eden are planted with every good deed." This wonderful statement reflects the way we can pick up the pieces for both our brokenness and our sins against others. Our blood may boil with jealousy and anger; we may rise up and strike, however, we must always remember that we are our brothers' keepers. The journey to reconciliation is in the relationship that we are willing to work at and heal with love. May our prayers cool the burning blood and may the peace of God take away our desire to strike another person. God is not far away at the times that we struggle with our brothers. God, the incarnate Jesus that we believe in as Christ, is beside us and within us as we work out our daily life. As Ronald Rolheiser writes, "The God of the incarnation has real flesh on earth and speaks to us in the bread and butter of our lives, through the things that have skin-historical circumstances, our families, our neighbors, our churches, and that borderline-psychotic friend who painfully reminds us that we are not

God."[13] We too must work out these relationships of daily life and come to communion with our brothers. We must be aware that caring for our brother may not be the plan of the day, but it is the plan of God. We may be surprised, and we may even need to wipe off some rocks and blood from a hard spill that causes us to be forced into actions, however our bond for one another is invaluable to humanity and the success of the world.

We may not be aware of it up front, however, yes, regardless of our similarities and differences, we are our brother's keepers. We may share a bedroom or a boardroom, have our names on the side of the same truck or live on opposite coasts and have completely different political beliefs, and remain our brothers' keepers. It may be distant or close, warm or respectful, but our brothers' keepers just the same. This is the product of Seth who took the crumbs of broken body and blood and with God gave us communion of the soul.

---

[13] _The Holy Longing_, Rolheiser, Ronald. Doubleday 1999. Pg. 95.

CHAPTER TWO

Esau and Jacob

The story of Jacob and Esau is a story of sibling rivalry. The twin brothers present as opposites in appearance, and temperament. However, deep within them is a similar fire for control and authority. The narrative unfolds as two boys who wrestled in the womb became bitter rivals and reconciled under the direction of God.

Their story reminds me of the bickering between children and the strain constant arguing between kids has on any parent. From the measuring of each helpings of food to perfect equality to taking turns for who is first to an activity can strain the nerves of a whole family. I have experienced separating children to help relieve the pressure of constant bickering however it doesn't always work. The two eventually come together and as a parent you hope it results in good. That may have been the benefit of having kids ride in different sections of the car to at least create a geographical boundary of a pillow, blanket, or another sibling none too pleased to be trapped in the middle of the war until hostilities cooled off. However, it usually seemed that an outside authority was needed to negotiate or order children to behave in at least a civil manner toward each other and possibly in a loving way for the sake of family peace. An outside influence is important to finding peace for sibling rivalries. The outside influence for Jacob was the challenges of his journey and of course his meeting with an angel on his journey to his homeland.

The difference between birthright and blessing comes to fruition in the story of Esau and Jacob. In contemporary times, the differentiations between these two distinct and real parts of inheritance are lost in a world that neither understands birthright and blessing nor gives them to their children. A child receives property ranging from financially valuable to simply sentimental. A will portions out to surviving relatives plots of land, vehicles, and personal possessions including jewelry. The birthright of ancient near eastern people reflected in the bible and in this setting was the patriarchal authority of the family and tribe. Besides a larger portion of all worldly possessions, the birthright made the receiver the priest and arbiter of the family. The blessing was a sense of God's protection for the receiver as well as valued honor from the leader of the family. The birthright and blessing do not appear in the language of contemporary wills and testaments.

The story of Esau and Jacob is that of both a sibling rivalry and that of parents who choose to favor one child over another. Esau was the first born of the twins and becomes the favorite son of his father. Jacob is the second born of the twins and becomes the favorite son of his mother. The sibling rivalry is fueled by parents who recognize characteristics that they value more than they value the two boys who are trying to outmaneuver one another.

As was the case between Cain and Abel, there was a sense that one brother cherished his relationship with God greater than his brother in the story of Esau and Jacob. Without even the prodding of his mother, Jacob desired the birthright that belonged to his brother, who in the culture of the ancient near eastern people, was the property of the first born in a family. The birthright is the opportunity to be close to God and serve his family as a priest. According to Heflin, "The birthright was a very important position within the Jewish family. All the needs of the family were taken to the Lord by the family priest. The relationship between family priest and God was one of great responsibility. The family eldest son, that accepted this responsibility, was revered for accepting this responsibility both within his family and the outside community. It was an honor to serve this duty and one that was taken seriously by the entire family."[14]

Esau trades the birthright to Jacob for some stew. The explanation for why Esau gives his birthright away to Jacob is because he is "very hungry." This rationale is an example of how Esau thinks about his relationship with God and the

---

[14] *Jacob and Esau: Birthright and Blessing.* Rev. Wallace H. Heflin, The McDougal Publishing Company, 1994, p. 11.

lack of value he puts on spirituality and family. It was a disconnect with God as Esau sees only the value of the material gifts that are his as the first son of Isaac. He values the items passed down from generation to generation as the sacred birthright not the spiritual gifts and responsibilities that Isaac will be passing on to the next generation.

From an anthropological standpoint, the Bible is reflective in this manner, "The Ugaritic treatment of the topic of progeny...The progeny is promised by divine annunciation and blessing. The biological process is supplemented with religious rites, incubation, direct divine revelation to the prospective father as to the necessary sacrifices."[15] Therefore, the stories found in the Bible follow the local customs and patriarchal lineages of the climate and culture. The tribal strength is delineated by this specific linear progression, and the stories or examples of this broken format are the legend and lore of the hero at each and every turn. The story of Esau and Jacob is a tale about the historic power of brotherly struggle from the beginning.

Esau and Jacob were the twin sons of Isaac. Because of nature, we know that only one child leaves the womb at a time. In the case of Esau and Jacob the squabbling brothers were fighting in the womb, Jacob grabbing his brother's heel in an attempt to be the first one out and be given the birthright of first born, however it is Esau who emerges first

---

[15] *The Bible and the Ancient Near East*, Gordon and Rendsburg, W.W. Norton and Company, New York, 1997, page 317.

from the womb. The squabbling of these two boys would last until one finally left the family unit. The reunion is the example of the transformation of childish bickering to sweet love enjoyed by brothers in old age.

The boys were as different as two could be from the same parents. Genesis 25:26-34 describes Esau as hairy and red and his brother not; Esau the hunter and Jacob the quiet one living in tents; Esau the favorite of Isaac and Jacob the favorite of his mother Rebekah, and Esau the simpler, salt of the earth character and Jacob the shrewd and cunning young man. From the beginning, Rebekah was troubled by the boys. When she petitioned to God for guidance the Lord answered with this reply in Genesis 25:23:

"Two nations are in your womb, and two people born of you shall be divided; the one shall be stronger than the other, The elder shall serve the younger."

The wiser Jacob desired the birthright would obtain it from his brother in Genesis 25:32 when a starving Esau comes back from an unsuccessful hunting expedition and trades his birthright to his brother for lentil soup and bread. Esau "despised his birthright." It could be said that Esau rejected his father in doing this but it could also be the rejection of the agrarian society in which he grew up. Esau was happier in the field hunting and living in the wilderness and not comfortable in the tent or in civilized society. He was wild and wanted the freedom of the second position. However, Esau did not want to break all ties with his father.

He did want his father's blessing. Being tied to the land and the business of farming may not have appealed to Esau, but he, as well as any male child in the ancient near eastern culture, recognized the blessing of his father. The blessing was the riches and authority to act in his name. The blessing was a part of the early religious connection that God would be with you and your household in the absence and passing of your father.

There is no question that Isaac was unsure as to who was in the room with him at the time the blessing was given out. However, God clearly knew that Jacob, not Esau was standing by Isaac's side and accepting the blessing of power and riches that was connected to the blessing. God knew that Esau was focused on the earthly riches and not the valuable spiritual blessings that were a part of the birthright and blessing that Isaac would give. Heflin elaborates for us, "When the Lord has spoken, His words cannot be recalled. Blessing which He has destined for us cannot be diverted. Let the devil do what he wants, he cannot hinder God's works in our lives. Nothing can take God's blessing from us."[16] God was setting the course for His chosen people and He was setting it on the head of Jacob and not Esau.

The setting of a blessing upon one brother instead of another could easily be construed as God intervening in a given situation. I do believe that God intervenes, that is the reason for many intercessory prayers, however our relationship with God is also a part of the experience of feeling blessed. The experience of blessings comes from dialogue with God and takes time and thoughtful inner

---

[16] _Jacob and Esau: Birthright and Blessing,_ Rev. Wallace H. Heflin, The McDougal Publishing Company, 1994, p. 22.

work. It is easy to find or chase after the exciting and interesting parts of life that entertain us and draw our time and attention away from God.. It is a challenge to maintain focus, demonstrate patience and maybe a better understanding of how the world works and how to build any relationship including one with God. The descriptions of Esau and Jacob in Genesis are not attractive. Jacob is usually considered a rogue, and he is however, there are unflattering qualities to the boorish Esau. If we search our inner lives just a little, we may find some Esau and Jacob within us as well. Norman Cohen captures this beautifully writing, "Modern psychologists have taught us that each human being has a multifarious personality which is made up of a variety of positive and negative tendencies. We tend to repress the negative components or 'Shadows' as Carl Jung labeled them, which consequently function as part of our unconscious. For some of us these inferior qualities have gained a stronghold and dominate our lives, though we may be unaware of them. Yet if we become conscious of our shadows, we have a chance to channel those tendencies toward constructive ends. This cannot take place, however, until we recognize the darker aspects of our personalities, admitting that these forces are real and present within us."[17] The story gives us insight to the battle that may rage within us, as we are our own twin or become aware of the shadows of our siblings. We are the "other brother" always under construction, always

---

[17] *Two That Are One, Judaism, Norman J. Cohen page 333.*

struggling within and beyond ourselves with our darker sides. We fight our laziness and deceit, our focus and our distraction. In the midst of all our personality battles, God calls us to be close and loved.

Esau may have been rough around the edges but he was not stupid. However, he may not have been fully aware at the moment of his brother's cunning and deceitfulness as well as his mother's desire to move Jacob ahead of him in the family hierarchy. Esau was easily trapped by Jacob because of his disinterest and lack of understanding of the family dynamic associated with children being the favorite of one parent or the other and this is how Jacob adds the blessing to the birthright to the list of honors he takes from Esau. Jacob, with help of his mother, donned a furry coat, which felt the same as his brothers rough exterior to his aging father. Jacob also possessed knowledge in the kitchen, which allowed him to prepare his brother's recipe for stew which Isaac asked for in his state of diminished health. This combination camouflage of body and culinary magic fooled his father's dulled senses and delivered Jacob the deathbed blessing from Isaac. Isaac, having confused Jacob for Esau based on the a furry coat he misunderstood as his eldest son's skin, and the taste of Esau's signature stew concocted by Jacob, gives Jacob the financial dominion of the estate and the patriarchal authority of the family. While Jacob has the blessing, he must flee his home from the danger of his brother's wrath.

So begins the story of Jacob, the second brother, who recognizes the importance of birthright and blessing and will eventually see the struggle of the "twin within" and hear God's call on his life to be a leader for God. The choice of Jacob, the second son and probably the least reputable, is an example of God's freedom of "divine election."[18] The divine oracle that John Edward Anderson describes in his text reflecting on Genesis 25:23:

The Lord said to her, "Two nations are in your womb, and two peoples from within you will be separated; one people will be stronger than the other, and the older will serve the younger."

is explained this way, "...does deception fulfill the divine oracle in 25:23? Gordon Wenham has raised this question but does not answer it head on. He writes that these narratives do in fact say something about God, but it is God's unfailing mercy that receives notice not how a history governed by God can unproblematically include deceptions as a method of fulfilling the divine plan."[19] God does not condone the behavior of Jacob. Nor does God condone our behavior that is hurtful and mean spirited in the world as well. God continued to call upon Jacob and God continues to call on you and me. The combination of listening and the providence of God is beyond the understanding of man and as such represents the call as an event outside human morality and behavior that we associate with gaining favor with God.

---

[18] *The Men and the Message of the Old Testament,* Peter Ellis, Mount Saint Alphonsus, N.Y., 1962, p. 14.

[19] *Jacob the Divine Trickster: A Theology of Deception and Yhwh's Fidelity to the Ancestral Promise in the Jacob Style,* Eisenbrauns, 2011, page 48.

The hard-headed Jacob departed his homeland, on the run from his angry brother. He escaped on a mission to find a wife in the land of his uncle. Along the way he was confronted by God at Bethel and given the same promise as Abraham to fulfill the covenant of the Lord. The man who laid his head on a rock to sleep, ascending the ladder to Heaven to speak with the Lord would be repaid good for bad and become the father of the twelve tribes of Israel with this promise in Genesis 28:13-14:

"I am the Lord, the God of Abraham your father and the God of Isaac; the land on which you lie I will give to you and your offspring; and your offspring will be like the dust of the earth, and you shall spread abroad to the west and to the east and to the north and to the south; and all the families of the earth shall be blessed in you and in your offspring."

The Bible is filled with second chances and opportunities given to men most unlikely to succeed. The story of Jacob is no different. He is considered by some to be an opportunist and scam artist, by others a patient man that outlasted his brother for both birthright and blessing. In either case, he is a man that came to recognize his sinfulness and still accept God's request to lead the nation. It would have been very simple for Jacob to respond to God's call with a litany of sins that would rule him out as the chosen leader of the tribe. Instead, Jacob faces his fears and faces his brother's wrath in accepting the leadership of a chosen people.

Jacob comes from an ordinal position that is subordinate, and he is unwilling to accept that from nature or his brother Esau. He spends a good part of the rest of his life confronting authority with mixed results. When he is successful with Isaac and claims the family birthright, he finds that at best this is a pyrrhic victory because he must flee to save his own life which is threatened by Esau. Jacob outsmarts both his father and Esau for a birthright he cannot utilize because of the broken trust he created with his brother. His life is in jeopardy, Jacob chooses to live out the birthright and blessing he has acquired as a stranger in a strange land. He has the earthly gift without the spiritual component that gives it value.

The same earthly ascension without the depth of soul fulfillment holds true for his relationship with Laban, the father of Rachel and Leah. Jacob labors the traditional seven years for the hand of Rachel only to discover that his veiled bride is the older sister, Leah, that he does not desire to marry. Jacob continues his servitude to Laban for the hand of Rachel. However, it becomes clear that the earthly pursuits of man never really provide the fulfillment that they initially promised and that Jacob's focus on the world leaves him wanting when his true guarantee is in the palace of his Heavenly Father.

The struggle Jacob faced with Esau seems to be a struggle within himself to honor the birthright and blessing or honor the pursuit of exterior advancement. The birthright and blessing that Jacob so desired is now recognized as a burden and deep responsibility that Jacob did not consider in his possible blind desire for both honors. The author Norman Cohen describes it this way, "The tension between our different sides and struggle to achieve wholeness is apparent in the sibling rivalries in the Book of Genesis. In almost every generation we are confronted by pairs of characters who, at one and the same time, are contrasting personalities but possess similar qualities and share some of the same reaction patterns. Cain and Abel, Isaac and Ishmael, Jacob and Esau, Leah and Rachel, Joseph and his brothers, all can be viewed as representing halves of a bifurcated whole...just as sibling conflicts are not irreconcilable, so too, the different tendencies in each of us can be integrated into a better functioning entity."[20] Jacob slowly learns the lesson that his struggles with others are also a struggle within himself. He is fighting on the outside with others and fighting on the inside with himself. He feels cheated and knows he cheats. He feels tricked and knows he tricks. The realization of our shadow self is embarrassing. It often takes many experiences to learn that lesson. However God remains patient with Jacob and remains patient with us. When we realize that God is close to us, we understand that God observes our mistakes and remains patient, finding places to invite us to wholeness and holiness, noticing the gift of life and expressing thankfulness for the new chances.

The story of Jacob in Haran with Laban throughout this portion of his life is one of leadership that is served. He clings to the vision and assumption that his gains are his based on hard work and determination. He does not witness the gift of his world as divine providence and connected to a much broader spectrum of humanity. It is only with Jacob's

---

[20] *Two That Are One, Judaism, Norman J. Cohen page 335.*

return home that he embraces his servant leadership role and the real birthright and blessing that justifies his life.

Jacob has one last hurdle to clear before going home. He faces God alone, as many people do in their lives, in a moment of truth. This moment sets the course for the people known as Israel. The irony of the story is that after wrestling with God, Jacob becomes the ultimate subordinate, allowing even his name to be changed. In the Biblical story (Gen. 32:28) "Your name shall no more be called Jacob, but Israel, for you have striven with God and with humans, and have prevailed," Jacob wrestles with God and is changed. "It is said that in youth, man wrestles with the devil and in old age he wrestles with God. The triumphant warrior that slays the dragon, moves up the company ladder, and strives to reach the pinnacle is replaced by the grandfather that is mellow, turns to the regenerative power found in a spiritual relationship with God and accepts his life as brief and with a purpose that is not self-serving but God serving. Jacob comes to grips with himself and his place in humanity that is a part of and not apart from God."[21] Jacob finally realizes to whom he is praying and worshipping. He connects with the awe in which he has existed but he did not choose to notice. He, as Abraham Cohen writes in Everyman Talmud; "is mindful of his precious endowment" and lives a "life influenced by the divine will."[22]

---

[21] _From Wild Man to Wise Man._ Richard Rohr. St. Anthony Messenger Press, 2005. pg. 147-148.

[22] _Everyman's Talmud._ Abraham Cohen. Schocken Books. 1995. pg. 78.

The lesson of Jacob is a lesson of theology. God is no longer "out there" and mixed up with the wishes and conversations with the wind. He is a very here and now, present and in contact being, that engages us in earthly matters. Robinson captures this along with others in his text, "God is not out there. He is in Bonhoeffer's words 'the beyond in the midst of our life,' a depth of reality reached, 'not at the borders of our life, but at the center,' not by any flight of the alone...For the word God denotes the ultimate depth of our being, the creative ground and meaning of all our existence."[23] This experience of physical turmoil holds an important historical benchmark for Jacob. This wrestling with God as an angel, becomes an important part of the ground of his being. When he wrestles with God, Jacob carries this experience throughout his life and it is an event that changes how he sees everything. Wrestling with God changes how Jacob lives his life and how he treats everyone else. When we struggle with God, when we run from God's command on our life and refuse to simply acquiesce, we join Jacob in this historic battle for control of everything. Jacob learns that wrangling with God leaves you changed. While he may have felt as if he won with the angel, the permanent injury changes everything. He walks away from that scrap completely changed. This physical injury to Jacob remains the reminder that God holds ultimate power and

---

[23] <u>Honest to God</u>, John A.T. Robinson, The Westminster Press, Philadelphia, 1963, page 47.

that when we return to humanity after fighting with God, we are changed. The very way we walk, as Jacob demonstrates with a limp, is changed. Jacob faces the road a different person. He is no longer the strident conqueror, but changed, humbled by the experience. Jacob meets Esau not as a cunning adversary, but with humility and having faced an intervention, softened, and aware of his sin and holding the importance of his relationship with his brother as valuable and sacred. We wrestle with God as well. We wrestle emotionally, spiritually, and physically with God through prayer, through illness, through decisions we make with how to live our lives. The struggles we have on the journey leave us changed. The tussles with God become the words we share with other people. The fighting with God, sometimes through tear-filled eyes, changes the places we live and the partners we decide to travel with on the path of life. Our daily life unfolds as a relationship with God that is connected to all people and all places and calls us to account for expectations and actions. I am reminded of my friends who have survived addiction and in recovery, speak differently. They hold the wound of the struggle with God to return to life and wholeness. God refuses to let them go to the peril of their addiction, and in recovery, there is something that is out of socket from the pulling and twisting that is noticeable. The suffering creates a different gait in the way they walk through life. Their stride is changed. The words they choose are filled with humility and care. They are aware of the pain and suffering they have endured and caused others to endure.

There is a tenderness in their heart. They have experienced what it means to be Israel. We too may know that feeling. God is as close as our very breath. This is what Jacob experienced, and we are invited to see that spark in every person and in the vastness of the universe.

God is in the stars as much as God is in the person sitting next to you and me on the subway. There is holy presence in the person hailing that taxi and in the fan of our least favorite sports team. In seeing this, we see that those people are our brothers. There is also a divine awareness that the spirit of God, the creator and created, circulates around us making the space we occupy holy and important. This belief brings us to this, "...love and its ultimacy are not projections from human love; rather our sense of the sacredness of love derives from the fact that in this relationship as nowhere else there is disclosed and laid bare the divine Ground of all our being."[24] The story of Jacob brings us to a place that says our true relationships with others are relationships with God. How we treat each other, is held within the heart of God. The holding of each of us in God's heart, is a reminder of our closeness, a connection that we should treat each person as if they are our twin brother. The reconciliation between Jacob and Esau reflects the connection that God holds our relationship in God's heart. God wants us to live together as siblings in loving kindness. God invites us to choose

---

[24] _Honest to God,_ John A.T. Robinson, The Westminster Press, Philadelphia, 1963, page 53.

relationship over acclamation of power, prestige, and position. The grace and forgiveness of Esau towards Jacob is the welcome of love we all desire when we have broken a relationship. Regardless of birthright and blessings, Esau demonstrates the behavior of the family priest, treating his brother as sacred and important.

CHAPTER THREE

Joseph and his Brothers

The story of Joseph and his brothers is a story about a young son who has a special gift. Joseph has two gifts really, both of which create friction with his brothers. The first is a special place in his father's heart, which leads to a special robe or coat that distinguished him from his brothers. The second is the gift of prophetic dreams. He is able to have them and interpret them for others. A unique gift calls for special care and awareness. The story of Joseph and his brothers is about his journey with his gift and its impact on his life.

Families in the United States today are much smaller than they have been in any other time in history. According to *U.S. News and World Report*, "the average family size in 1900 America was 4.76 in comparison to the 2000 census that puts the number at 2.59."[25] The article did not provide

---

[25] *U.S. News and World Report, "An Amazing Story." Roger Siman and Angie Cannon,. August 6, 2001, Pg. 5.*

specific reasons affecting the reduction in the number of children families are having in the United States. However, there should be consideration of the conflicts that large families have amongst siblings. This type of conflict was found in the story of Joseph and his brothers, who were none too happy with his dreams which represented a pecking order that put Joseph on top and his older brothers playing second fiddle.

You can imagine as a brother of two older siblings, which one would have wished that a child's parents may have considered a smaller family than the three boys that made up our nuclear group. You can imagine that fighting over everything from toys to the last French fry drove our parents as crazy as it drove each of us as we jockeyed for both position and attention in the family unit. It did not occur to me to get rid of those brothers at any time. However, one cannot be as confident that those brothers did not consider selling the author into slavery or at least to the circus for the many antics that caused turmoil and tears during childhood. I imagine the brothers of Joseph having those same fantasies about their brother not being around. Joseph's brothers actually acted on those impulses of evil and by the grace of God, worked to save their lives.

The dynamic between siblings always carries a sense that the older is in a place of authority. I imagine that if you have an older sibling, you can recall moments when that sibling was given authority over you in the absence of your parents. As a child, I recall the many times I heard mothers call out to their eldest children to "watch out for your brother," whether it was to chase after the ice cream truck or walk to school. However, imagine if a parent called out to a younger sibling with the same message. If you can imagine that exchange on the road in front of your house with a mob of children holding coins for the ice cream man, it would be hard to picture them without mouths wide open. It would be hard to picture the older sibling not burning with anger on the inside and red faced on the outside. The ego is an easily bruised body.

If we can step outside that dynamic of peer to peer relationship and examine the conversation in a differing light, we can see the ego in a safer position. This is the lens for human interaction that plays out in the Temple with Jesus and the religious leaders. Notice that his age plays a role in affecting their ego and not the message. The dynamic with Joseph and his brothers runs a parallel course.

The Bible contains a story in the Gospel of Luke that may offer some light on the challenges of ego as it relates to age and authority. As Jesus sits in the Temple discussing theology and religion with the great scholars of the day, the Bible texts explain that the religious leaders marveled at the twelve year old boy. "How could a boy speak so wisely?" they must have imagined. It is more straightforward for an adult to marvel at the wisdom, knowledge, or skills of a youngster when there remains a separation between that youngster and the ego of the onlooker. The marvels of the boy passing through town are not intimidating, threatening, or frustrating to the religious leaders because there does not exist a gravity to events that cause them any discomfort. As we know from later incidents in the New Testament, these same words lead to the arrest and crucifixion of Jesus because the words carry the gravitas that becomes threatening, intimidating, and frustrating for the religious elite. The change in both situations is not the words spoken by Jesus but the relationship of the listeners. The words have become closer, not in sound, but in spiritual resonance and that causes the conflict with the clergy of the time. The dynamic has changed and therefore the meaning has changed.

The attack on the ego is certainly not confined to the chief priests found in the Jerusalem Temple. Instead, ego is shared by all people. And there is no more significant damage to ego than when a younger sibling outperforms his or her elder brother or sister. The slight can come physically, mentally, or emotionally. However when it happens, it stings with brandish that few have the depth of soul to accept.

The first conflict between Joseph and his brothers came in the example of a gift. Jacob, the father of Joseph, made him a long robe with sleeves according to the story found in Genesis 37:2-11. The jacket was different and more lavish then the robes given to his Joseph's brothers. This created tension between the brothers. Joseph's brothers were jealous. This was followed by dreams that had the brothers of the family bowing in homage toward Joseph both as sheaves and as celestial bodies treating Joseph as a royal and the family as his subjects. These types of revelations are presented as far outweighing the usual sibling competition and boasting that made for turmoil within the farming and shepherding families of the Hebrew Scriptures. The conflicts between siblings in scripture come to conclusion in many ways. The competitive nature of Joseph and his brothers created an alliance among the brothers who felt slighted and offended by the words of their brother. As allies, they began to scheme and decided to sell him, throw him in a well, and have him sold off in slavery.

Joseph, the son of Rachel, the most favored of Jacob's wives, was one of the twelve sons of Israel. God has given him the gift of having dreams and interpreting dreams that have prophetic power. Joseph, being a young man, took this gift and did not use it in the most God serving way. As a seventeen-year-old boy, he flaunts the gift before his very jealous brothers. In Genesis 37:6-7, he boasts: "Listen to this dream that I dreamed." knowing that this would anger his brothers. Joseph can interpret dreams, which is explained later in Genesis, but for now, he flaunts the talent to frustrate and annoy his brothers. This leads to their decision to sell him to the Ishmaelites.

Joseph loses his position of favor the moment he leaves his father's house. Through slavery, deceitful practices toward him, and prison, he comes to find a world without guarantees and where his humility is required for survival. It is at this time that Joseph recognizes his talent as a gift from God and how that gift provides vocation as service to the Lord through feeding the masses of humanity. Joseph prophesied in Genesis 41:25-30:

"Then Joseph said to Pharaoh, "Pharaoh's dreams are one and the same; God has revealed to Pharaoh what he is about to do. The seven good cows are

seven years, and the seven good ears are seven years;
the dreams are one. The seven lean and ugly cows
that came up after them are seven years, as are the
seven empty ears blighted by the east wind. They are
seven years of famine. It is as I told Pharaoh; God has
shown to Pharaoh what he is about to do. There will
come seven years of great plenty throughout all the
land of Egypt. After them will arise seven years of
famine, and all the plenty will be forgotten in the land
of Egypt; the famine will consume the land.' "

It is at this time that through experience and humility Joseph finds a vocation matching his ability to understand and read dreams. It is as David Brenner refers to when he describes vocation. Joseph finds a place for his gift that is "...a purpose of being that is grounded in God rather than in himself..." and "...is a call to serve God and his fellow humans that fits a distinctive way that fit the shape of his being."[26] When Joseph finds his confidence in God and not just himself, he is open and receptive to the full use and value of the gift he has received. He then recognizes his vocation as manager of the food for pharaoh is a call for greater action beyond Egypt as found in Genesis 41:41-43.

And Pharaoh said to Joseph, "See, I have set you over all the land of Egypt." Removing his signet ring from his hand, Pharaoh put it on Joseph's hand; he arrayed him in garments of fine linen, and put a gold chain around his

---

[26] *The Gift of Being Yourself.* David G. Benner. Intervarsity Press, 2004. pg. 96,97.

neck. He had him ride in the chariot of his second-in-command; and they cried out in front of him, "Bow the knee!" Thus he set him over all the land of Egypt.

This was an opportunity to use his gift for good beyond the service of his master. Joseph recognizes that his gift of "seeing," understanding dreams and using that information not to harass his family but to offer some valuable good beyond the people within earshot. The premonition of the famine gives him the power to store food in the present to survive the coming tragedy.

We read in Genesis 41:53-57 just how this unfolds,

The seven years of plenty that prevailed in the land of Egypt came to an end; and the seven years of famine began to come, just as Joseph had said. There was famine in every country, but throughout the land of Egypt there was bread. When all the land of Egypt was famished, the people cried to Pharaoh for bread. Pharaoh said to all the Egyptians, 'Go to Joseph; what he says to you, do.' And since the famine had spread over all the land, Joseph opened all the storehouses, and sold to the Egyptians, for the famine was severe in the land of Egypt. Moreover, all the world came to Joseph in Egypt to buy grain, because the famine became severe throughout the world.

Joseph opens his heart and answers God's call to feed His people. Joseph uses his power of dream interpretation to save the grains that will feed the Egyptian and quite possibly the many kingdoms, tribes, families, and people who faced starvation at the hands of this lean time.

However this is very challenging for him to maintain. We are often directed to think of the dreams that Joseph shares with his brothers as an example and illustration of his expected authority and leadership in the family. And the scripture pronounces that for the reader with vigor as well as the fundamental reflex of his brothers to do Joseph harm. A deeper look from Yoram Hazony provides a different interpretation. "Joseph's dreams reflect what the brothers might otherwise have guessed: that Joseph sees them not as shepherds, not as nomadic and independent agents and therefore as fundamentally equals; but as farmers, members of a vast structure of earthly power in which their lives depend on the protection of rulers who provide sustenance and arms."[27] This dream and it's presentation to his brothers was more significant than simply a vision that his brothers would bow down and be ruled by him, Joseph was seeing a hierarchy that his father had spurned to inherit the spiritual understanding of God. Jacob saw the dangers of urban life (in this era) that tied people to one another in negative fashions. The experience, he feared, would make him less desirous to be present to God and a prayerful, thoughtful life. As Jacob feared, Joseph discarded the agrarian life and turned his attention to the business of commerce and political relationships. These relationships seeped both into the family unit and beyond the family to create a pressure to place God behind the state and municipal authority under the guise of the greater good.

---

[27] *The Philosophy of Hebrew Scripture*, Yoram Hazony, Cambridge University Press, Cambridge, 2012, page 122.

This luxurious and safe life is unfolded in the narrative of Joseph and the Hebrew people as they move away from their shepherding and nomadic lifestyle, to the civilized experience associated with Egyptian nation status. The original dream of the binding sheaves that gathered and bowed down found in Chapter 37 of Genesis was the dream prophesied that survival of the tribe is associated in the long term to Joseph's placement as a lord and leader in the court of the monarch and the hunger for grains available in the dominion controlled by the king and administered by Joseph.

While Joseph is honored with authority to control the assets of the Pharaoh, he is not free to move about, of his own accord, serving in an individuated captivity if you will, which becomes more of a house arrest, and finally an exalted position of authority and power. This is far from solitary confinement at the beginning, and he becomes less interested in escaping or even asking for his release and the release of his family. It seems evident that Joseph is favored by Pharaoh and chooses to remain far more than being forced to remain a part of the Egyptian hierarchy.

Consider the coming and going of Joseph's brothers. They are outsiders and come to Egypt in the same fashion as others in search of food to relieve the famine. Upon completing their mission, they are free to leave. This challenges the reader to consider that Joseph may have a similar opportunity. However, he chooses to stay, naming his children in the Egyptian fashion and lifestyle. He ignores the past in the same way the butler forgot him in jail. However, the brothers of Joseph have learned a lesson. This is explained by Stanley Brice Frost where he wrestles with the encounter between Joseph and his brothers concerning the stolen items. The brothers could easily leave Benjamin behind and save themselves as they left Joseph to be sold into slavery, but they do not, "But when they are again challenged with the same decision whether to further their own welfare at a brother's cost, they refuse to save themselves by abandoning Benjamin to slavery in exile, and it is then that Judah rises to truly noble heights: 'Now therefore, let your servant, I pray you, remain instead of the lad as a slave to my lord; and let the lad go back with his brothers' (Gen. 44:33). It is then, too, that Joseph, assured that they are not cruel and mercenary as they were on that impulsive, hate-filled day so many years before, discloses himself to them as their brother ready to forgive. These are indeed men as we know them today, capable of much evil and yet also of great good."[28] There is a lesson to be learned in these exchanges that Joseph doesn't learn. The human exchange is somewhat lost on him, even though he forgives his brothers he is unable to follow their example of leaving the comfortable zone for the honorable path.

Joseph stands in the tension of turning away from his father's path, expectations, and God. Hazony captures this again writing, "Among the great commentators were those who claimed that Joseph's behavior in Egypt was flawed, criticizing his adoption of Egyptian customs; his

---

[28] _Patriarchs and Prophets,_ Stanley Brice Frost, McGill 963, page 38.

willingness to permit his service to Egypt to bring dishonor to his father; and the arrogance of rule that disfigured his character even as an adult."[29] There is frustration and anger in Jacob that Joseph turned away from his culture, heritage, and connection to God, for a life of Egyptian luxury. This reaction of Jacob is hard to face for the believer, since there is a direct connection between Joseph's actions and the families rescue from starvation. The dreams are also God inspired. I think Jacob would have appreciated it if Joseph made every effort to leave Egypt after the famine was over. If the family could not leave, I think Jacob would rather be in conflict with Pharaoh than in cooperation with his captor. This eventually happens to the Hebrews.

Following the famine, Joseph breaks with God, ceases to follow the dream and remains in the house and service of the Pharaoh. The close of the famine represents the close of that vision of the dream associated with Pharaoh. The original dream interpretation returns to view from Chapter 37. If Joseph remains in Egypt, his brothers will bow down to him as the appointed overseer for Pharaoh as well as a life confined to empire and not nomadic tradition. The dream becomes a warning to leave Egypt and return to their original home, thereby restoring the Hebrew people to their right relationship with God. Joseph's refusal to recognize the dream as a warning

---

[29] *The Philosophy of Hebrew Scripture,* Yoram Hazony, Cambridge University Press, Cambridge, 2012, page 123.

dooms the people to eventual bondage. He loses sight of his purpose and is unable to remove himself from the confinement that was originally forced upon him that he now chooses or forces upon himself, "...Joseph is always concerned with the interest of his current master. And in this tireless pursuit of his master's interest, Joseph is forever persuading himself that he is doing what is best for his people at the same time."[30] Joseph enjoys wealth, power, and prestige as the dean of the Pharaoh's cabinet. He is no longer the youngest brother who is tormented and abused, but the person who pulls the levers and pushes the buttons to make the Egyptian Empire an economic powerhouse of the region. Joseph becomes a prisoner of his own success, fearful of losing power, prestige, and authority in the house of Pharaoh and forgetting the house of his father Jacob and God who has called him not to restore the fortunes of his people but simply to survive the famine and return to a life that follows a rhythm of grace.

The question of whether the ends justify the means is one that challenges humanity across time and land. The decision to hold God in abatement while we prepare ourselves, our families, our legacy is difficult to dispute in a commercialized and economics based era and society. However, the lesson of Joseph portrays an opportunity to self-examine when our riches or means have moved

---

[30] _The Philosophy of Hebrew Scripture_, Yoram Hazony, Cambridge University Press, Cambridge, 2012, page 124.

beyond surviving the famine or hardship years and become more of a warehouse of commodities and funds that do not point to lean years, but compiling riches where enough is never enough. This becomes a fear based existence and clutches a zero-sum economic system where any gain of the objective individual is a loss to the subjective self.

The call of God is an ordering of ourselves to have God remain first in our lives. The story of Joseph, just by its very nature of record in Genesis before the Book of Exodus and the Commandments brought forth by Moses, begins by putting God ahead of all other thoughts and understandings. The second commandment instructs us "to have no other gods before me." That command includes the gods of power, prestige, and property. The Decalogue reminds us to be aware of these other gods that are constantly struggling for position in our lives. The life of Joseph is one that warns that in the moment he left his father's side he was struck with a lostness that could only be replaced with satisfying and pleasing other father figures, masters, and lords. The experience of Joseph is a temporal struggle to solve the wound of disconnection from the father in some manner and the ways we try to salve the wound, or find ways to fill that empty space. Richard Rohr describes men with the father wound, "They grew up without a good man's love, without a father's understanding and affirmation. So they hunger for it , and they search for it from teachers and coaches, ministers and scout masters, and any older man who will offer it to him. Later in military or business world, they seek to be approved by their superiors in exactly the same way. They become the good team player, the good soldier, who would do anything...so long as it meets with his approval."[31] For Joseph, it was work that he used to escape the feeling of loss, the feeling of neglect, the danger associated with his brothers and the trust or lack of it they put in his heart. The only way that Joseph seemed able to find solace was in pleasing his new supervisor and chaining that to the desire to bring his family to comfort and safety.

Therefore, the lesson of Joseph is to find the hole in our heart, the parent hunger we may crave and recognize that which is trying to filling it. There is no treasure in the world which will fill the empty void of the absence of acceptance by our missing parent. Try as we might, each step beyond enough, is a step toward our ruin and our bondage in the recurring system. The hole may only be filled with love and tenderness. The hunger only satisfied by the longing being quenched, the keeping of covenant and relationship with God and one another. Our hearts are filled with relationships, deep, whole, and complete. God remains that parent figure always willing to love, always willing to listen, always prepared to be with us in our life.

---

[31] *From Wild Man to Wise Man.* Richard Rohr. St. Anthony Messenger Press, 2005. pg. 67.

CHAPTER FOUR

Moses and Aaron

The story of Aaron and Moses is one of brotherly loyalty and love. The story of two brothers who are of one blood, separated at birth and by circumstances, they come together to free their family and God's chosen people from slavery. This is the foundation of the story of Moses and Aaron.

A partnership is a challenge for any two people who are working toward a common goal. This is no different for siblings. From the first time you agree to shovel a driveway together to earn money in the winter to cutting the lawn in the summer, brothers struggle with partnerships. The question always arises as to who will be the leader and who will be the follower. It seems that in any hierarchy, someone needs to be the boss and someone needs to be the employee, and that is usually where ordinal position comes into play. The eldest generally holds the top position. That is not the case for Aaron and Moses, and the results benefit more than these two brothers but an entire nation of people. The story of Moses and Aaron is the narrative of an elder brother following his younger brother, giving us comfort in our struggle.

Moses is the younger brother of Aaron. This is not one of the most well-known parcels of information provided for in the Bible. While we don't have an enormous amount of information about either brother, we find that in Exodus 7:7 Moses was eighty years old and Aaron eighty-three when they spoke to Pharaoh.

The relationship between Moses and Aaron is unusual to say the least. From scripture and history, we know that Moses was not raised with his brother Aaron. Instead as the book of Exodus explains, Moses was sent into the river Nile by his mother because Pharaoh was planning to murder the next born sons of Israel to reduce the population. Moses' mother (Jochebed) places him in a basket and floats him down the river to the unsuspecting royal family in hopes they will take pity on the child. Moses is found by the Pharaoh's daughter in Exodus 2:6, she recognizes the child as a Hebrew who has been cast into the water instead of facing murder at the order of her father, and decides to bring the boy into the family. Pharaoh's daughter has the child removed from the water and takes him into the family as if she bore him herself. The actions of Pharaoh's daughter weigh on her choice of the name Moses, in its Egyptian sense is "to beget a child," however the Hebrew definition of Moses is "he who draws up." The narrative later demonstrates how Moses is able to fulfill the divine derivation of this name by not only drawing Israel through the Red Sea, but out of the bondage of Egypt and in the direction of the Promised Land. In the meantime, Moses grows up a part of the Egyptian hierarchy.

The attendance of Moses in the royal court provides him with the rare opportunity for a Jewish boy to have the academic, legal, and religious doctrine in addition to understanding and awareness of the royal education system of Egypt. Moses learns and has the same experiences that any child living in an exclusive setting would enjoy. If we can picture a present day royal education, we can imagine the training and instruction that Moses was exposed to as a prince of Egypt.

The Book of Exodus is unclear about the specific age or time when Moses learns of his Hebrew lineage. There seems to be great turmoil within Moses about this revelation. He sees the Hebrew people not as faceless robots working for him but kindred souls sharing lineage, familial bonds, and personal connections. Moses learns that his family is mixed into the people who are slaves to him. This new knowledge weighs upon him, and when he sees an Egyptian taskmaster beating a slave, he reacts by murdering the overseer. Moses escapes to the desert to hide from the authorities for his crime. He arrives in the house of Midian.

The wisdom of the House of Midian serves Moses well. The father in law of Moses provides sage advice to his son in law in organizing the life of the community, and is valuable later for the Hebrews while they journey to its promised destination. Moses now has the knowledge and experience from two core bases of learning.

Moses utilizes his foundation not for the Egyptian state, but instead he uses his knowledge and preparation for justice and truth to organize the Hebrew people. He does not use it to support a state that values loyalty to Pharaoh who emphasizes inhumane treatment of a people forced to servitude. Moses applies his knowledge and experience to lead the Hebrew revolution against Egypt, navigate the wilderness, maintain order on the forty year journey, and deliver the Hebrews to the edge of the Promised Land.

Aaron and Moses remain separated geographically. The collaboration between these two brothers would seem impossible, however nothing is impossible with God. This disconnect between the brothers would continue beyond their basic upbringing. Following his falling out with the Egyptians and the Hebrews, Moses would leave Egypt and live his formidable forty years Midian with his father in law.

The narrative shifts when Moses is confronted by God at the burning bush. Moses brings his entire history of birth, Egyptian life, man on the run, welcomed traveler, and loyal son in law to this meeting with the God of Abraham, the God of Isaac, and the God of Jacob at the burning bush.

The burning bush is a moment from the Book of Exodus that draws us into a very interesting story. The burning bush is an incredibly small miracle based on

physical appearance. However, the message is powerful. The God who makes the world, universe, and all that it contains chooses a rather small sign to call the new leader of His chosen people to draw them out of bondage.

In Exodus 3:1-3, we learn how Moses hears God's call, Moses was keeping the flock of his father-in-law

Jethro, the priest of Midian; he led his flock beyond the wilderness, and came to Horeb, the mountain of God. There the angel of the Lord appeared to him in a flame of fire out of a bush; he looked, and the bush was blazing, yet it was not consumed. Then Moses said, "I must turn aside and look at this great sight, and see why the bush is not burned up."

But what if the burning bush was not just simply a sign but an assessment of Moses' willingness to hear the voice of God. Rabbi Lawrence Kushner describes how Moses needed to be intoned and possess the vision to stop and notice the burning bush. Then Moses needed to be still long enough to focus on the bush to determine that it was not being consumed by the flame. Once God was sure that Moses was not distracted and was ready to listen, he began to speak.[32] Moses possessed the vision of the bush that others did not. The others needed the huge miracle, the separation of the Red Sea, the Pillar of Fire. Moses is tuned in enough to follow the small miracle, hear the small voice of God. Moses is able to do this because he is not wrapped up in work of his worldly father but of his Heavenly Father. Moses is open to the greater commission to lead Israel out of bondage.

In the presence of the burning bush, Moses notices and is frightened by the miracle. However, we learn that his faith is strengthened and he moves closer to God. We

---

[32] *Jewish Spirituality: A Brief Introduction for Christians, Lawrence Kushner, 2001, p24.*

read in the work of Nahum Sarna, "His initial encounter with God is a terrifying experience, a reaction shared by other biblical characters. Later, in the course of his career, by dint of his intimacy with God, Moses is so emboldened as to request a glimpse of the Divine Presence."[33] This growth in faith and assurance is a reoccurring theme in the narrative. Not only does Moses grow in faith, so does Aaron. Aaron grows in faith when he hears the call by God to meet with Moses before he enters Egypt. The parallel story is the growth in relationship between Moses and Aaron. The brothers were separated for a majority of their lives and yet the call of God on them individually brings them together as prophets of the Lord, and as brothers who serve God to bring the people held in bondage to freedom.

Harkening back to the introduction of the chapter, it is interesting that the shared countenance of Moses and Aaron, allows Aaron to hear the Lord too and go into the wilderness to meet his brother. They are separated at the birth of Moses, yet something deep within keeps them attached, and the voice of God draws them both out of their comfort zones and into uncharted leadership positions to lead the Hebrew people from slavery to freedom and eventually a monarchy of their own. Aaron had just enough of the foundation that Moses had to make the connection with God's whisper.

---

[33] _The JPS Torah Commentary: Exodus,_ Nahum M. Sarna, The Jewish Publication Society, New York, 1991, page 15.

Aaron, at the outset of the Book of Exodus does not escape to the desert as Moses does but is forced to continue in the painful labor of oppression in Egypt and be enslaved with the remainder of the Hebrew people. The bondage described by Sarna in another texts is described in this fashion, "The Israelites, under the oppression, were conscripted to build the cities of 'Pithom and Ramses' and it was from the latter site that people started their march of liberation out of Egypt."[34] The remnant of Hebrews who were in the region who were once a part of a larger community, possibly the Hyksos (who invaded the region many years earlier), but were now forced laborers with partial autonomy."[34] They were allowed to have leaders and Aaron was a part of the leaders in the community.

Aaron was from the Levi lineage according to Exodus 6:16-20. An elder son, Aaron was considered a leader of the Levi tribe and would provide Moses the door of introduction to the leaders of Israel that was still in Egypt. Exodus 4:14 establishes that Aaron is also an eloquent speaker and will be happy to meet you. Lastly, the brother of Moses is historically considered a man of even bearing and righteousness. The Rabbi Hillel from the first century made famous the saying "Be of the disciples of Aaron, loving peace and pursuing peace, loving one's fellow man and bringing them nigh to the Torah." [35]

The important and powerful Aaron is contacted by God to meet his brother in the wilderness. Would Aaron, having

---

[34] _Exploring Exodus,_ Nahum M. Sarnum, Schocken Books, New York, 1986, page 10.
[35] _Who's Who in the Bible_, Readers Digest, 1994 pg. 7.

known the jeopardy he was putting his good name into have met with his outcast outlaw brother? We need to remember that Moses fled and did not just leave to "go find himself." He was chased out of town after murdering an Egyptian who was beating a Hebrew slave. The text gives no reason for the beating, which may have been for a transgression or for sport. In either circumstance, Moses felt the indignity of it, the suffering in the heart of the slave and the injustice of the act. While Moses was tethered to an Egyptian upbringing, he was aware of his Hebrew roots and this tension boiled into anger in defense of the cowering slave. This was a serious crime and forty years may not have been long enough to be away for the memory to fade.

Moses we know became a shepherd for his father-in-law, Jethro, the priest of Midian. This is a far cry from the stature and authority of a boy brought up in the house of Pharaoh. There is a feeling deep within Moses that one might imagine he must have believed that he was destined for greater accomplishments then tending sheep in the wilderness. He realizes that he is of noble or royal background. Richard Rohr describes this in his workshop "True Self, False Self," where he explains that each of us in family communion with God has at the core of our DNA God and that the deepest us is God. "That when God breathed into the nostrils of Adam he breathed life into every living thing, and in so doing our human bodies contain divinity which truly makes us members of God's Kingdom and His royal family. The sense that we are made for a great service and princely work is really true."[36] We are all the lost child of a great King with inheritance that is abounding. The King is God and the inheritance is the Kingdom of the Lord.

Aaron goes to the wilderness to meet his brother because he was ordered forth by God. He arrives to find Moses who was given a plan by God to free the Hebrew people. Moses was a reluctant prophet, however he is growing in faith with God and recognizes the meeting with Aaron as a confirmation to the words of the Lord. This is a plan Aaron, the Levites, and the rest of the tribes for that matter, had not attempted or tried. How could he now risk life and name on this brother he hardly knows? I am sure Aaron was not happy being a slave, however approaching Pharaoh at his brother's side and asking for freedom, the freedom of the slaves who were integral to the economy of Egypt, was similar to asking to butcher the entire society, was quite a favor for Moses to ask after not seeing his brother for forty years. If we consider this in a more contemporary setting, the request goes a little beyond a long absent brother showing up at your doorstep and asking to borrow the car to run to the grocery store.

Immediately, the plan does not go well. Pharaoh is furious and decides to punish the Israelites by taking away the straw used to make the bricks. Moses and Aaron find themselves very unpopular at the very beginning of their mission with Pharaoh and the Hebrew people. Directly,

---

[36] *True Self, False Self, Richard Rohr, Workshop, 2000*

Moses angers his Hebrew brethren as they are forced to produce the same number of bricks without the straw provided by Pharaoh in Exodus 5:20-21.

As they left Pharaoh, they came upon Moses and Aaron who were waiting to meet them. 21 They said to them, "The Lord look upon you and judge! You have brought us into bad odor with Pharaoh and his officials, and have put a sword in their hand to kill us."

This forces them to works exponentially harder than before and certainly makes the work more taxing and stressful. Aaron is embedded in the Hebrew culture but Moses is not. That is what makes the message difficult for both groups as Sarnum describes, "Moses conveys the message to the Israelites, but it falls on deaf ears. Crushed by the cruel bondage to which they are subjected, and given the awesome power at the disposal of the Egyptian state, the people understandably regarded the utopian declaration as being utterly irrational. It would henceforth be the task of Moses to convince them that what seemed to be irrational would inevitably be reality."[37] This added much more stress and angst in his life and the relationships he had with the leaders of the Hebrew people. No one was exempt from the harsh reactions of the Pharaoh in response to the challenges of Moses spoken through Aaron. One can only imagine life back at Aaron's house when he returned for dinner at the end of the day. It must make for tense dinner conversation. Every wife has a family and I am sure Aaron's in-laws were

---

[37] _Exploring Exodus,_ Nahum M. Sarnum, Schocken Books, New York, 1986, page 66.

more than waiting for him when he got home. I can't imagine that he was not being chastised by those closest to him for the direction in which the revolution is going for the Hebrews. They are all suffering and must feel that Moses is doing more harm than good for their cause. Yet Aaron stays by his brother's side. He doesn't give into the popular culture. He doesn't go back to Pharaoh and apologize "Gee my brother is a nut; let's go back to the old rules." Instead, he is steadfast and supportive.

Moses continues to listen to God's instructions to meet with Pharaoh and offer relief to the Hebrew people. In the face of Pharaoh's refusal, God unleashes the plagues and Moses and Aaron continue to negotiate and warn Pharaoh of the impending doom overshadowing the Egyptian kingdom. The conflict persists until the last plague, the death of the all the firstborn of Egypt, except those marked for protection. The night is the first Passover. These are words from Exodus 12:29-32,

At midnight the Lord struck down all the firstborn in the land of Egypt, from the firstborn of Pharaoh who sat on his throne to the firstborn of the prisoner who was in the dungeon, and all the firstborn of the livestock. Pharaoh arose in the night, he and all his officials and all the Egyptians; and there was a loud cry in Egypt, for there was not a house without someone dead. Then he summoned Moses and Aaron in the night, and said, "Rise up, go away from my people, both you and the Israelites! Go, worship the Lord, as you said. Take your flocks and your herds, as you said, and be gone. And bring a blessing on me too!"

***

Moses draws the people out of slavery to freedom. The name of Moses is a play on words. While the daughter of Pharaoh focuses on the name having a source that refers to being a son and drawing up from the river, God uses this "drawing up or out" etymology to assign Moses the task of drawing the Hebrew people out of bondage and lead them in the journey towards the Promised Land.

Ten plagues later, the Jews are set free and Aaron is as triumphant as Moses in this end to enslavement. Moses and Aaron stick together in the family business: the liberation of an entire people.

In the end, the story of trust and love and reaching a common goal between Aaron and Moses is parallel to the movie "The Blues Brothers." They too are on a mission from God, and eventually liberate an orphanage trapped under economic enslavement. The line, "We are on a mission from God," makes one wonder that what other missions are worth undertaking and completing.

This story of brothers is an example of a partnership, divinely guided and resulting in the strength of the bond we call brotherly love. The mission of salvation that these two brothers carry out stretches beyond themselves to the entire family of the children of Abraham.

The great mission of Moses is to return to Egypt and set the people free. Moses is reluctant, as are all the people God calls to service, and he begins to provide a litany of reasons why he is not the good choice. God then allows Moses to be strengthened by leaning on his older brother Aaron for support, guidance, and partnership.

Moses, the second born, is sacrificed to God as the one who loses his life to lead a life of sacrifice to God and

His chosen people. Moses was then and still remains an integral part of the Jewish religion. He is intimate with God in the way only a first son would be intimate with his father. Moses holds the position of grandeur and respect amongst other sons of God the way younger siblings would see an older brother and the relationship with a father in early agrarian culture. Moses is *Moshe Rabbenu* "our teacher." No other character from scripture possesses the same level of closeness to Yahweh that Moses enjoys.[38] The inheritance of Moses is a fortune that any first son would be jealous to possess. Moses was humble in his acceptance of the gifts given by the Lord and to the end was the servant and provider for the people of Israel who were gifted with the chosen status of God.

Moses becomes a good brother and partner with Aaron. Moses hears the word of God to meet his brother to pronounce the end of bondage and exodus of the people. Aaron eventually makes errors, allowing the people to make a golden calf to worship while Moses is on Mount Sinai. However, Moses forgives his brother for his lack of fortitude in his absence. Just as Aaron believed in God, had faith, and served Moses in meeting Pharaoh to carry out God's plan to deliver the people from bondage, Moses honors Aaron and God with a heart that asks for forgiveness. It was Moses who burned hot with anger when he killed the Egyptian overseer, now he is changed by God to a person who cherishes relationship and forgives. I find this a valuable lesson in human growth and brotherly love.

---

[38] *Who's Who: the Old Testament,* Joan Comay, Oxford University Press, 1993, p.12.

CHAPTER FIVE

David and his Brothers

The story of David is a narrative of one man's overcoming adversity to succeed. David is the youngest of huge family and is undervalued from the beginning. He finds his strength and courage in God and uses the tools of his life to serve the Lord and become king. All tools can be used wisely but need to be treated with great care. A tool may be dangerous if it is not treated with respect. The strength of conquest is David's tool and he loses power over it. The narrative of David gives us insight into how to treat our God-given talent with respect and dignity. The talent belongs to both us and God.

The story of David brings to mind the image of a person with unlimited potential. I think we all know someone who was incredibly talented and did not live up to their potential. We may have wished we had their size, their skill, their intellect as we measure it against our limited aptitude. Every element of life can be a gift or burden. That being said, it is much easier to consider that capacity from the outside.

Therefore, witnessing someone not reach their potential is hard for us yet we cannot understand the challenges of the one we are judging. I can picture people I thought had not done all they could do under my limited knowledge, only to learn more later about them and their struggle. However the observation and the later deeper analysis hold great opportunities for our personal growth.

We are introduced to David in books that do not bear his name. The Books of Samuel reflect the transfer of the mantle of prophecy from Eli to Samuel and the bloody transition of kingship from Saul to David. The Books of Samuel follow a young prophet, who was dedicated and given to the Temple by a mother who prayed to God for a son. The mother of Samuel, Hannah, prayed and promised God that if she was given a son, this child would be dedicated to the Temple, offered to serve as a sacrifice of gratitude from a pious woman. Samuel was given in service to the Temple by his mother and served Eli amongst Eli's sons. In the course of work, Eli knew that his sons, who were younger, wiser, and knew better, had not served the Lord well. Samuel remained committed to the Lord. He did not take advantage of his position or authority. Instead, Samuel's service was honored by God.

" Now Eli was very old. He heard all that his sons were doing to all Israel, and how they lay with the women who served at the entrance to the tent of meeting. He said to them, "Why do you do such things? For I hear of your evil dealings from all these people. No, my sons; it is not a good report that I hear the people of the Lord spreading abroad. If one person sins against another, someone can intercede for the sinner with the Lord; but if someone sins against the Lord, who can make intercession?" But they would not listen to the voice of their father; for it was the will of the Lord to kill them. Now the boy Samuel continued to grow both in stature and in favor with the Lord and with the people." (1 Samuel 2:22-26)

There was no doubt that this upset Eli and because of this, the word of God came to the ears of Samuel and not Eli and not the children of Eli. In chapter three we learn that God calls out to Samuel in the middle of the night. Samuel hears his name called and runs to Eli, who is the only person around, to ask what he needs. After three such encounters, Eli advises Samuel to respond to the voice simply stating, "Speak Lord, your servant is listening (3:9)." These three calls to Samuel from God, resulted in the fourth that becomes the transition of prophecy from Eli to Samuel and begins the shift away from Eli's family to Samuel and away from the kingship of Saul to the selection, anointing, and fruition of the prophecy that David would be king.

As the newly chosen prophet, Samuel is called upon to satisfy the desires of the people in selecting a king. He selects Saul and when God's favor leaves Saul, Samuel is again tasked with finding the king. He sends him to Bethlehem to meet Jesse, the father of seven sons. This lead to a review of the boys of Jesse.

"Jesse made seven of his sons pass before Samuel, and Samuel said to Jesse, "The Lord has not chosen any of these." Samuel said to Jesse, "Are all your sons here?" And he said, "There remains yet the youngest, but he is keeping the sheep." And Samuel said to Jesse, "Send and bring him; for we will not sit down until he comes here." He sent and brought him in. Now he was ruddy, and had beautiful eyes, and was handsome. The Lord said, "Rise and anoint him; for this is the one." Then Samuel took the horn of oil, and anointed him in the presence of his brothers; and the spirit of the Lord came mightily upon David from that day forward. Samuel then set out and went to Ramah." (1 Samuel 16:10-13)

From the lot of Jesse's boys, who run from the tall to the powerful and handsome, Samuel selects the youngest and least likely. The shepherd is the outcast of the community and of course the outcast of the family. David is assigned the worst job in the family structure; yes Samuel selects the runt of the litter. Yet, David is selected by Samuel. Samuel hears the voice of God to anoint David. Human eyes cannot see what God sees and while the predictable choices of appearance and ordinal position would direct Samuel in one direction, God has other ideas. David is chosen for his depth of faith. We learn throughout the Hebrew Scripture that reflects on his life, that David's words and actions originate in prayer. David asks God for guidance and understanding, prophetic visions, and strategic information to serve as king.

David is also incredibly human. He demonstrates the strengths and weaknesses of the human condition. Throughout the story of his life, David gives the reader the good, the bad, and the ugly of the human personality. He is flawed and he is real. He gives us chances to adore him and look at him in utter disappointment. These swings in character may be why he is so well known and honored in Judaism as well as Christianity.

David is the Cinderella story, with more plot twists than any other in the Bible, he is both hero and anti-hero, which makes him, to say the least, an incredibly approachable human. "Overlaid by a system of rewarded piety and punished defection, a system embodied by the prophet Samuel, David's drama enacts forces of ambition and destruction, love and betrayal, volcanic strivings and equally powerful appetite. The story manifests an undying wonderment at the spectacle of a beautiful boy who pursues his course and flourishes as a dominant hero, and then becomes an angry old man."[39]

David is the underdog at the beginning and never sheds this persona. As we may certainly think of Sylvester Stallone's "Rocky" as the lovable nobody who overcomes adversity as an underdog to reach the heights of sports greatness, David is much less a climber who uses far less heroic manners to overcome the obstacles. As we learn, "This is one meaning of the folktale of the Clever Younger Son: the conventional hierarchies and bonds are imperfect. Repeatedly, the order of things must be supplanted by guts or brains, in the interest of survival. The dark, primitive thread of necessary violation runs through the elaborate tapestry of David's career…"[40] David uses whatever means are necessary to reach his objective. Some of those objectives are admirable and others are simply dishonorable. He refuses to be pigeonholed as a one dimensional character in a bad novel with predictable actions and dialogue. And in most instances, he pauses, asking God for guidance, asking

---

[39] _The Life of David_, Robert Pinsky, Nextbook Schocken, New York, 2005, page 6.
[40] _The Life of David_, Robert Pinsky, Nextbook Schocken, New York, 2005, page 14.

God for deliverance, begging God for reconciliation. The relationship with God points toward the desire to reach the pinnacle of his existence, to serve as God's anointed king over the chosen people. The road is bumpy and rough throughout the voyage, however David eventually serves as the monarch of a holy people.

In the same manner that pizza is delivered to our homes, so too David serves at the lowliest of causes delivering bread and cheese to his brothers at the battle with the Philistines. Instead of dropping his parcels at the door and escaping with a tip, David engages in the festivities and receives a reprimand by his brother. And so the nosy youth begins his questions about who will stand up to the bully on the playground. Who will allow the name of God to be trashed?

David is emotionally and spiritually confronted by the soldiers and the king who operate from a consensus that Goliath who is big and strong can only be defeated by a bigger and stronger person. The soldiers and the brothers are familiar with the rules and it becomes clear that David needs the rules explained to him, for he is young and foolish or as they say unmarked by the difficulty of life. He was considered a blank slate. "For if Saul is the one asked for (Sha'ul), David is the one who asks. Beginning with his first spoken words (1 Sam 17), over half of his speeches are built around questions, real or rhetorical, more than ninety in all -questions that are at once the screen behind which he hides and an expression of the riddle at the core of his persona."[41]

---

[41] *The English Bible, King James Version, The Old Testament, Herbert Marks, W.W. Norton and Company, New York, 2012, page 503.*

However, instead of a blank slate, David was more impressionable to ask questions and search for answers that others would not consider valuable. He realized through questions and answers that Goliath could not be defeated in the conventional manner. The conventional wisdom would not suffice in defeating this giant of the Philistines. David even tried on the armor of the King and recognized that it did not fit his body or his way of thinking about the world. Instead, as smooth as his young skin, he drew five smooth stones to him to face the enemy and defeat Goliath. David was cunning and ruthless. David caught Goliath by surprise in his appearance and tactics and struck him in the head with a stone. He knocks the giant unconscious and then jumps upon him like a tike only to demonstrate his level of contempt by beheading the monster with Goliath's very own sword. This is truly gory but surprising in the same moment.

However, it seems that the foreshadowing of David's behavior and depth, as well as breadth of actions, are aligned with his position in the family.

As any younger brother knows, it is a pecking order of being last that results in a lineup of adversaries to reach the position of equality at the table. The youngest sibling grows up under the voracious appetite of older brothers and sisters who need their own punching bag, pawn, or gopher to ease the labor of being the oldest. And as we know, the worst jobs are at the bottom of the hill, the youngest finds themselves at the bottom of same said hill.

If you can imagine the harassment, the teasing, the pushing around in a family, the smallest is often the one who is relegated as the easiest to persecute. If you have three brothers to pick on you and beat you up, imagine double that number, and well before the existence of any protective elements.

The story begins with the selection of responsibilities at Jesse's homestead. David holds a position that would certainly be considered practically outside the acceptance of the household. Just as the prodigal son was sent to tend the swine by his brother, David is sent to perform the duties of a hired hand, not a noble son. In the hierarchy of the house, David is at the bottom of the barrel, bruised and battered; but he refuses to give up.

This historical narrative delivers us to the battle of Jews against the Philistines. The soldiers of Saul are all immense in size and stature, but none as big as Goliath. In the eyes of David, one mountain looks no different than another. One challenge, no more arduous or dangerous than another. And having survived the shellacking he takes from seven older siblings, one giant does not seem as formidable an adversary to David as it would for another man who never had to battle against the rest of the family for basic necessities.

David uses the cunning, the skills, the surprise that have saved him from destruction at the hands of seven siblings, on an unsuspecting Goliath. The toolbox of survival skills are what David employs to defeat Goliath. David uses strategies of surprise, refusal to accept the status quo, and faith that God will provide him with a "nothing to lose" courage to defeat the mighty warrior.

For David, the moment with Goliath is repeated again and again throughout his life. He is undervalued and misread by friend and foe alike. He is sized up by adversaries, both men and women and thought of as weak and unsure because of his many questions. However, they underestimate the skills of David and this works, to some extent, to his advantage. For those who love him, who stand in the in-depth assessment of David, he marvels us as king, leader, warrior and lover. The heroic vision of David can capture us in this way, "...David spent his years as kind of a pirate, as a rebel leader, and eventually as chieftain over his loyal troops as a turncoat follower of the Philistine king Achish. And everyone who was in distress, and everyone who was in debt, and everyone who was disconnected was gathered to him. And he became captain over all of them."[42] In contrast, his siblings remained in the house of Jesse, obedient to the hierarchy structured from the nomadic tribes, to the agrarian communities, and eventually the urbanized civilization norms.

David's use of those strategies, that wisdom, that heart and soul, was often used for personal gain and swelled the ego of David. When David used himself for the glory of God, his life truly pleased the Lord. The honorable use of gifts is the incredible challenge of the youngest sibling, to recognize that all power and honor is to be given to God and to use the hard fought gifts in God's purpose. For each victory, each accomplishment, each accolade is so easily marked as one's own hard work, one's own determination, independent and self-satisfying. The

---

[42] _The Life of David,_ Robert Pinsky, Nextbook Schocken, New York, 2005, page 35.

triumph is the danger and experience that David swung in his pendulum of life. He took full credit at some moments and gave all glory to God in other moments. The constant switching of poles make David such an attractive figure while simultaneously being undesirable.

The twin peaks of David's personality attract and repulse those around him. His family remains distant for a good portion of his life, however other people enter his orbit and find him an irresistible public figure. The dislike of Saul for David is practically unquenchable. And the love or attraction of others are nearly as committed to David. Foremost in finding him attractive was Jonathan, the son of Saul who was closer than any brother and Jonathan's sister Michal (David's wife) who protected him from her father. They are joined with holy men like Ahimelech and kings like Achish, all of which serve as brothers to David, supporting him during difficult times. The times when he was attractive to others were when his heart was pure, he was following the signs and words of God, he was humble and obedient. The heart filled with the goodness of God was easily recognized by the people he came into contact with on his journey to be king. David spoke with earnest care for others, with actions and compacts of trust and reconciliation, and with an authenticity that his heart was moved by God.

David demonstrates spiritual brilliance at moments, heeding God's word to negotiate, fight, and serve the needs of the people. By doing this, he is recognized as not only a leader, but a faithful child on God. The brothers who once scoffed at his every word and action, follow him on his quest to become king. In 1 Samuel 22, the entire family unit comes not only to his aid but to take up arms with him as they work to seat him as the ruler of the Kingdom. This reassuring experience must have given David confidence in a struggle that often left him bewildered and unsure. So often he was on track to restore the holiness of God to the Kingdom followed by setbacks that nearly broke his back and the back of the rebellion. I can imagine David second guessing himself and considering a less arduous way of living out his life.

This is the mindset of nearly every person I know on the spiritual journey. It is two steps forward and one step back. The ego holds us so tightly, and our success determines so often our interior dialogue and unconscious selection of the next challenge. We begin to play inside our own arena, selecting jobs, activities, and even projects at work that come easy and result in the most accolades and attention.

The applause captures us and becomes a limiting factor. David became enthralled by what he did well and began to lose sight of the purpose of life to live and love in communion with God. The more he grew in stature, the smaller he became in his outward view of God's call upon his name. This lack of self-assessment is captured masterfully by Franciscan priest Richard Rohr, "Most of us are never told that we can set out from the known and familiar to take on a further journey...Shocking and disappointing, but I think it is true. We are more struggling to survive than to thrive, more just "getting through" or trying to get to the top than finding out what is really at the top or was already at the bottom."[43] While we are called by

---

[43] _Falling Upward_, Richard Rohr, Jossey Bass, San Francisco, 2011, page xvii.

God to live in a fullness of our enthusiasm, we mistook that enthusiasm for worldly success and do not grow tools and strategies of our youth to their fullest potential, instead mimicking them or morphing them into small jobs that have exterior dividends.

Our gifts and graces are given to us freely and with love from God. We are invited to use them in the ever-expanding experience that we have with God through our relationships with others in the present moment. The gifts given to David had application in his youth and had application in his old age; however he never seemed to see that those strategies bore meaning for larger and more significant uses in relation to God.

One item that King David is most recognized for is his defeat of Goliath. He draws from the courage he experienced in protecting the family flock as well as the strength and ingenuity of the wilderness to fight for justice. David learns that to defend truth, the entirety of your faculties must be harnessed to thwart evil. He is able to do this in his defeat of the giant.

However, at some moment, David must travel further down the path and find that God calls us to work for justice, but the fight does not come at the point of the sword. The fulfillment of justice exists in alternative means of compassion, reconciliation, and peace. David continued to lead revolution and counter-revolution throughout his life and neglected to see the mercy he showed Saul as a mercy to change the minds of the world. He also could not find mercy for himself to be still with God. David lived as if always on the move, always on the hunt, always searching and not finding what he was looking for in his life. The endless physical and emotional rummaging brought success but never the peace David described.

He comes to this tension. We all come to this tension really, in our lives. We are no longer young and not quite in the grave. We still believe that peace and justice are good, however, the pursuit system for lack of a better description does not really exist. We can continue to slay dragons or enemies, or move further up the corporate ladder or purchase the vacation home, or lead raids against our competitors to win some success, yet the justice and peace we crave eludes our existence. We are the lion, caged in the zoo, pacing back and forth, unable to satisfy our urges and needs and unaware of the confines of the situation. We are caged and ignorant and unable to take the necessary steps to relieve the stress. So we aimlessly succeed and do not feel satisfaction. This is what led David into trouble, and holds the same for us; the inability to be satisfied yet we are using the well-crafted techniques and strategies that result in outward positive recognition.

This is the beginning of Jungian theory of the "Second Half of Life." This is, as Rohr describes as, the "crisis of limits" whereby the old script will not give us the rest and reassurance that we desire and bring us to wholeness and closeness in life. We must retool if you will or repurpose our tools to match the second half of life. David searches but cannot find the new grip upon the means he has to engineer peace and harmony with God and life. And so, he is stuck. And sometimes, so are we.

The second half of life is the time that we renegotiate the way we face the world. No longer fighting with the passion that easily spills over to anger but with the gentleness of wisdom and generosity, and generativity, the using of our skills, our wisdom, our open hearts to shape the world. It seems that whenever I look out the window, our nation is at war. As a previous combatant myself, the call to arms, to stand shoulder to shoulder with my brother on the battle lines, has been the bugle that signaled my presence. Today, I believe the clarion calls me not to the front, but to the places at home where wounded and fatigued warriors return and need a differing call to arms, a call to be by the shoulder of fellow warriors who desire comfort and reconciliation, hope, and warmth as they assimilate to the post-war world or at least their post-war world or at least their post-war world.

The harp that David used to soothe Saul before the battle, may be refashioned to be the music that settles the racing heart of one who returns home in search of comfort from the chaos that is battle. There is an astuteness of engaging those who are unsettled from a place of shared experience as well as honest dialogue for the inherent goodness within. No two people have the same experience in war, nevertheless there is common ground to engage the deep work of healing. We are not called to heal one another, but to walk together along the road of life. We are called to support each other, sooth each other, smooth the rocky road for each other, as siblings both biologically and spiritually to reach our spiritual destination.

The street smart and shrewd thinking and behavior of David who stood toe to toe with his mocking brothers and surprised Goliath at the Valley of Elah, may well be the same strength and strategies needed to stand in unity and alliance for the disenfranchised and disconnected of society. The subtle words of goodness and support may create a layer for loving peace and justice and the end of hostility with others and more importantly within himself, or within oneself.

As the youngest of many children, the younger or youngest sibling brings forth a unique perspective to the relationship with one's brothers as well as life and faith in God. The devices and contrivances that pave the way, from simply survival to thriving reflect a continuum that may not be required or acquired by older and more substantial siblings. The challenge of this youngest brother is to use those implements wisely, see them as gifts and graces from God, and reconstitute them for the age of wisdom and generative living. The experience of adolescent struggle at the hands of elder siblings is the path that allows us not to be turned away from building the Temple for the Lord but inviting us to use our own hands and soul to refashion our small home into the mansion of God's eternal life.

As children of God, may we look deeply into the mirror of the soul to evaluate our motives and actions. As we pause long enough to see deeply and hear clearly, I pray we recognize the difference between living to succeed for ourselves and living to succeed for God. The best use of our minds, bodies, and souls, are to play big and to exhaustion for a loving God and not seek the small easy victories of an always hungry ego. As we go deep in that faith journey, may the fruits of that work truly provide us with the well water that quenches our thirst and enlivens us to greater life in God.

CHAPTER SIX

Andrew and Peter

The story of Peter and Andrew was one of mutual support where never were two brothers so very different but yet so valuable to the success of the other. Andrew and Peter were night and day. Peter the younger, as we know of course is the one on whom Jesus would build his church through that Rock. Andrew was the one who brought the people into the doors of the church. The great introducer, Andrew introduced Peter to Jesus and the development of this tight group resulted in the nexus of the Christian Church.

The story of Andrew and Peter reminds me of two boys who lived in my neighborhood. They lived up the street. A large family with two brothers much younger than the rest. The whole family was tight, but these two younger brothers had a different bond. They finished each other's sentences, and always knew where the other was on the field or the court. These two brothers lived off the "no look" pass. They played every sport as if they shared a common consciousness. That was a great partnership between brothers that everyone could appreciate.

Unlike other brothers previously examined in the text, Peter and Andrew have a partnership. They were intricately connected by their work as fishermen. As the Gospel of Saint Luke offers, the brothers worked together, "The previous night's fishing, which had produced nothing involved a partnership of two boats. Until very recently, this was how fishing was organized in the limited fishing area of Tabga; without a partnership, conflict could easily arise."[44] The Sea of Galilee is also the Sea of Tiberias, the Lake of Gennesaret, and the Sea of Kinneret. The body of water has these names because of the many lands that have shores that the water washes upon their coast. Therefore, each group, region, tribe was committed to controlling a portion of the property, but more importantly a portion of the fish that are within. It becomes quickly apparent that the Sea is contested property and the only way to maintain any viable business is to be in collaboration with someone else. In the same manner that families remained united to work the land and harvest in cooperation, the fishermen were working in a categorically similar manner, pooling the resources of boats and hands to remain an active business. The Gospel of Luke Chapter 5:1-7 provides,

Once while Jesus was standing beside the lake of Gennesaret, and the crowd was pressing in on him to hear

---

[44] Nun, M. "Cast Your Net Upon the Waters: Fish and Fishermen in Jesus' Time." Biblical Archaeology Review 19, no. 6 (1993): 48.

the word of God, he saw two boats there at the shore of the lake; the fishermen had gone out of them and were washing their nets. He got into one of the boats, the one belonging to Simon, and asked him to put out a little way from the shore. Then he sat down and taught the crowds from the boat. When he had finished speaking, he said to Simon, 'Put out into the deep water and let down your nets for a catch.' Simon answered, 'Master, we have worked all night long but have caught nothing. Yet if you say so, I will let down the nets.' When they had done this, they caught so many fish that their nets were beginning to break. So they signaled to their partners in the other boat to come and help them. And they came and filled both boats, so that they began to sink.

Fishing as Nun describes is the intersection of expertise to use of heavy nets as well as the experience with a multitude of nets to harvest the varying types of fish, "Although the indigenous fish population of the Sea of Galilee consists of 18 species, only 10 are commercially important"[45] required a multitude of fishing techniques, coordinated supports, and nets to use as fishermen evaluated the school of fish below the surface. There were different nets for different parts of the day and different techniques and strategies that the fishermen used to survive in the Sea. The scripture describes the importance of the relationship between the

---

[45] Nun, M. "Cast Your Net Upon the Waters: Fish and Fishermen in Jesus' time. "Biblical Archaeology Review 19, no. 6 (1993): 48.

brothers to work several hours and in concert to be effective fishermen. The Gospel also provides a glimpse into the relationship that they must have with their neighbors as the Zebedees are called upon in one version of the story to assist in the heavy catch.

The coordinated work is also reflective of the differing nets that are used by the fishermen. Each net was constructed in a differing style and each net was employed differently to harvest the fish. Lastly, the fishermen must remove the fish from the net for preparation for market.

The example most often used is the seine net. "The seine, or dragnet is the oldest type of fishing net. Until recently, it was the most important fishing method on the lake. The seine net is referred to in the Hebrew Bible and the Talmud. The seine is essentially a dragnet...Its footrope is weighed with sinkers...is spread 100 yards from the shoreline...and hauled to the shore with towing lines...The whole team would then harness themselves to the nets and pull them to shore..."[46] The fish are then examined for cleanliness and value before the process is repeated.

This is relentless work, the kind of vocation that takes dedication and determination. Besides the obvious challenges of many fishers on the water, the swimming of schools of fish was not a simple mathematical equation. The fishermen were required to study the currents, the seasons, the weather, and the tides to determine the proper

---

[46] *Nun, M. "Cast Your Net Upon the Waters: Fish and Fishermen in Jesus' time." Biblical Archaeology Review 19, no. 6 (1993): 51.*

application of fishing skills in the water. Fishing required seamanship as well, using boating strategies to steer and navigate the waters of the Sea. They also had to negotiate the relationships with others parties close to them on the Lake as well as the people who they tethered to in partnership in adjoining boats as well as the person who was on the boat with them.

So clearly, the partnership between Andrew and Peter, or Simon as he is known before meeting Jesus, must be one of balance and space, pace and understanding. The one must take action as the other must be passive, one must be urgent while the other must be patient, one must take the reins of steering the vessel, as the other remains almost docile, awaiting the action of the fish that nearly capture themselves in the net.

And the dynamic between Andrew and Peter could not be more ingrained in this relationship. We learn quickly in the Gospel of John, Chapter 1:35-42:

The next day John again was standing with two of his disciples, and as he watched Jesus walk by, he exclaimed, 'Look, here is the Lamb of God!' The two disciples heard him say this, and they followed Jesus. When Jesus turned and saw them following, he said to them, 'What are you looking for?' They said to him, 'Rabbi' (which translated means Teacher), 'where are you staying?' He said to them, 'Come and see.' They came and saw where he was staying, and they remained with him that day. It was about four o'clock in the afternoon. One of the two who heard John speak and followed him was Andrew, Simon Peter's brother. He first found his brother Simon and said to him,

'We have found the Messiah' (which is translated Anointed). He brought Simon to Jesus, who looked at him and said, 'You are Simon son of John. You are to be called Cephas' (which is translated Peter).

The patient and reflective Andrew held his tongue and attention for the entire day as he listened to the words of Jesus to recognize the mark of the Messiah. He immediately brings his brother Simon, the one who is the person of action, the one who lacks the patience and demeanor for spending the day, but this younger, "other brother," immediately impresses himself upon Jesus as a man of strength, who he will ask to lead his church someday very soon. "When Jesus addressed Simon by name, He accepted him just as he in fact was, an impetuous and impulsive fisherman...No doubt he was uncouth in his conduct, unrefined in his manner, and no stranger to rough language...yet underneath he was idealistic, perhaps even impractical...This is the man who on that Galilean day stood in the presence of Jesus with no particular merit or advantage in either vocation or temperament."[47] This is the brother, the partner, the rock that he called as first among disciples for the new church and shepherd to the Kingdom of Heaven. In the moment, Jesus sees the entirety of Simon, his past, present and future. The love of God, so powerful in the power of seeing and making believers. "The true nature of a

---

[47] _Peter: The Rock Man_, Frank G. Carver, Beacon Hill Press, Kansas City, 1973, page 11.

thing is the highest that it can become. That is what we really are, the highest that God has chosen us to become."[48] Jesus calls Peter to be the brother who is the partner of the Apostles, the partner to work in the Holy Spirit and the partner of the Christian Church's future. He calls him to transcend his work on the boat and shore to work in bold evangelism for the Way, the Truth, and the Life.

For Andrew, the story does not come to an abrupt conclusion or a conclusion at all with the words of Jesus to change Simon to Peter. In the same fashion that the brothers were partners in the fishing industry, they remained partners in the work of ministry and mission for Jesus Christ. This was a place to draw out new skills and strategies that reflected the foundation of the partnership and the fishing vocation. This is explained well by Michael Coyner, "Fishing in the Sea of Galilee involved a cooperative effort of one person rowing the boat in circles while the other person carefully let down the folded nets into a large circle that would be drawn together to trap fish. That is why the request of the risen Christ to 'cast your net on the [other] side of the boat' (John 21:16) was such a strange instruction that yielded such unexpected results. It would be like asking someone to shift from doing a thing right-handed to doing it left-handed. Long practiced teamwork would be difficult to change, but it is typical of Jesus to call disciples to try new patterns for better results. Part of what Andrew and the other

---

[48] *Peter: The Rock Man*, Frank G. Carver, Beacon Hill Press, Kansas City, 1973, page 17.

early disciples left behind was a sense of paramount individualism. Instead, Andrew was part of a growing team of followers of Jesus."[49] Andrew leaves behind his old life as a fisherman and retools his skills and thought process to serve as a disciple of Jesus Christ. As the older brother, he is incredibly humble and committed to Christ and that is demonstrated wherever Andrew is recorded in the story.

For example, in the Gospel of Saint John 6:4-9 we read,

Now the Passover, the festival of the Jews, was near. When he looked up and saw a large crowd coming toward him, Jesus said to Philip, "Where are we to buy bread for these people to eat?" He said this to test him, for he himself knew what he was going to do. Philip answered him, "Six months' wages would not buy enough bread for each of them to get a little." One of his disciples, Andrew, Simon Peter's brother, said to him, "There is a boy here who has five barley loaves and two fish. But what are they among so many people?"

I imagine this is Andrew circling the boat theoretically, recognizing the need and remaining a steady member of the partnership looking for the guidance of his stronger younger brother through experience but turning those watchful eyes and ears to Jesus. When Jesus is able to turn those few morsels into enough food to feed thousands, Andrew is again strengthened in his faith and his role in this new partnership.

---

[49] *The Andrew Paradigm,* Michael J. Coyner, Abingdon Press, Nashville, 2012, page 31.

Andrew demonstrates his strength not in demanding a larger role or in expecting a name change. He accepts his position with a sense of honor for fulfilling his calling in the group of Apostles. The author Michael Coyner captures this beautifully by writing, "Even though Andrew started following Jesus before his brother, and even though Andrew played a key role in introducing his brother to Jesus, Andrew was known as 'the brother of' the more famous Simon Peter. Andrew apparently accepted that role which this book is calling the role Lead Follower, without objection. At least we do not have stories of Andrew quarreling with Simon Peter or others about his importance. We do not have a story of Andrew or Simon Peter making a special request for a preeminent position with Jesus (like we have with James and John). We don't have any stories of Andrew criticizing Simon Peter for his denials of Jesus, for his lack of faith that made him sink like a rock when he tried to walk on water, or for his apparent inconsistencies. It is hard to imagine that two brothers like Andrew and Simon never argued, but the absence of such information in the Gospel leads us to assume that Andrew was able to take the secondary role without complaint. Perhaps Andrew followed Jesus by leaving behind not only his nets but also his ego."[50] The willingness to leave behind the past is the strength of Andrew in the brotherly partnership and the place in the group of disciples. His letting go gives his brother space to excel at the fishing trade and his expanded internal growth to let go of his ego allows him the wisdom to live as an apostle.

---

[50] *The Andrew Paradigm,* Michael J. Coyner, Abingdon Press, Nashville, 2012, page 35.

The partnership between brothers and fishing families, the fisherman's unwritten creed of maintaining the fraternity of workers of the sea, is similar to the consistent expectations of Jesus when he calls Peter to be that sure person, reliable companion, and spiritual anchor for the group of twelve. The road however is littered with errors on the part of Peter who struggles with this responsibility as the powerful fisherman crumbles under the weight of the task in Mark 8:32-33

He said all this quite openly. And Peter took him aside and began to rebuke him. But turning and looking at his disciples, he rebuked Peter and said, 'Get behind me, Satan! For you are setting your mind not on divine things but on human things.'

Luke 22:34
Jesus said, 'I tell you, Peter, the cock will not crow this day, until you have denied three times that you know me.'

Matthew 26:40
Then he came to the disciples and found them sleeping; and he said to Peter, 'So, could you not stay awake with me one hour?'

John 18:26-27
One of the slaves of the high priest, a relative of the man whose ear Peter had cut off, asked, 'Did I not see you in the garden with him?' Again Peter denied it, and at that moment the cock crowed.

When Peter denies Jesus three times, he on several levels denies the very core of his being. As a fisherman and the anchor to partnership with his brother and closest friends, he exposes himself as not worthy to hold up his end of the bargain. The surety and cockiness of Peter is exposed as just that, a person who cannot be relied upon to be the brother who maintains his reliable part in the fishing trade, one who cannot maintain their place on one end of the net, to steer the boat strong and true, to mend and clean the nets.

The second, and obviously most important piece, is the denial of the Lord, the refusal to be the reliable rock that Jesus has called him to be as the one who will stand firm in the faith; as the one who has been trusted with healing miracles, transfigurations, and mysteries that others have not shared in as a privilege to his closeness with Christ.

These are the conflicting emotions and incongruity of words and actions that Peter faces within himself as he crumbles in the portico. This action is the mirror that he looks into as he reflects the life he has been a part of over the past three years and the moment of truth when he is challenged by the onlookers to the suffering of Christ at the hands of the Temple authorities.

Jesus knew both the recklessness of Peter and the reliability of Peter as a fisherman in the fishermen culture. His goal was to move that to his life in Christ. "Calculated obedience is no obedience. There has to be recklessness about it a refreshing anticipation of what Almighty God will do as we prove Him. Then we find out how much his ways are above our ways and his thoughts higher than our thoughts."[51] This is the Peter that Jesus sees and foretells unbeknownst to Simon the fishermen who is unaware that when Jesus calls him to be a "fisher of men" it is greater than any salty sea and torn hands and fingers have experienced at the pulling of the ropes that bind the net, but a genuine partnership of relentless and reckless commitment to a life in Jesus Christ. As Frank Carver describes, "At Jesus' feet, wet with the sweat of toil and the spray of the sea, his face almost in the fish, was a strong man, a torn man with conflicting emotions. Out of the almost annihilating breakthrough of the presence on the holy into Simon's feeble moral existence came the reassuring reconciling word, 'Do not fear' with its daring promise for such a man."[52] This is the place when the searing fires of baptism mold and shape Peter in the same manner that they mold and shape us. We no longer are justified by self but justified by the never-ending love of God.

The grace comes to final fruition when Jesus asks Peter three times if he will feed the sheep that belong to Christ. The question and answer is the moment when the fisherman sees the grander interconnectedness of who he thought he was, who he became, and who he has always been. The solid rock of God. Peter is engaged as Frank Carver writes, "The wrong of our past can no longer

---

[51] _Peter: The Rock Man_, Frank G. Carver, Beacon Hill Press, Kansas City, 1973, page 29.

[52] _Peter: The Rock Man_, Frank G. Carver, Beacon Hill Press, Kansas City, 1973, page 33.

imprison our spirits with its crippling tentacles of guilt and frustration. The right of our former life beguiles us no more with its pretend inadequacy for the will of God is in the present. Jesus has become our future."[53] That is the light that Peter stands in at the beach eating fish and that is the light we stand in, as we come to real communion with God. When we, in a sacred way, come to the table, encouraged to feast on the love of Christ, and are called to feed others through our partnerships as siblings in the family of God.

The action of Peter is one of unusual confidence. "Our faith, when Jesus calls us to action, must leap beyond our limited analysis of the situation to an implicit confidence."[54] Peter now stands in the deep understanding of who he is as human being and follower of Christ. He recognizes his weakness and strength. He sees the image of the rock, not as something that Jesus referred to in the past, but as the person he will become in the brightness of the resurrection. The work of a fisherman-the anchoring power, the reliability, the assuredness-was simply training wheels to the life with Christ. In this moment, Peter is born into his name and into a new life in Christ. The strength and courage he is given to lead the church, chiseled and hewn in the times with Jesus, he is sculpted from the most raw materials that existed before in his life. He is the other brother, who by virtue of raw materials is transformed into the Apostle, the disciple of Christ that partners with us all in our journey.

---

[53] _Peter: The Rock Man_, Frank G. Carver, Beacon Hill Press, Kansas City, 1973, page 38.

[54] _Peter: The Rock Man_, Frank G. Carver, Beacon Hill Press, Kansas City, 1973, page 30.

In the same manner that Peter comes to Christ in the rawest of natural resources, we too come to Christ as the granite and marble prepared to be formed by the living God. We arrive at the door to knock, feeling so sure of our power and authority, expecting God to simply smile and put us to work in the "doing" we know so well. We are flattered by the grand welcome and the royal treatment. We, in the same manner as Peter, pass through unaware of the trying and testing that will make us the disciple the Lord intends to make of us. And it is in this trying, and learning, that in defeat and loss, Christ remains steadfast, teaching us to be steadfast. "The fact that Peter had followed Jesus, even 'at a distance into the courtyard of the high priest,' is a great tribute to his moral courage and his sense of loyalty to Jesus. The point is not that Peter was a coward at heart and that Pentecost transformed him into a brave man. The point was that he was an extremely brave man, the flesh at its best."[55] The implication is that Jesus calls us to a deeper relationship beyond our body and mind to the heart of the matter. "What Peter's denial demonstrates is the complete inadequacy of the flesh at its strongest before the demands of the cross."[56] Christ does not want a fisherman, but a fisher of men. Peter is slow in learning this in relationship to his brother who experiences a more linear growth. The lesson of Peter is the lesson that

---

[55] *Peter: The Rock Man*, Frank G. Carver, Beacon Hill Press, Kansas City, 1973, page 66.

[56] *Peter: The Rock Man*, Frank G. Carver, Beacon Hill Press, Kansas City, 1973, page 67.

some brothers arrive as partners to their relationships with their siblings, and God provides even greater partnership and brotherhood as well as sisterhood, in the broader sense of the word. We can develop as Peter develops into the partner, reliable companion and brother that is the special gift and grace that Peter had and others have as well. Peter is a great partner, and we too are called to be great partners in our faith journey, bearing witness to others of the life and light we know only in Christ. We are called to partnership at the foot of the cross, with humility and love. This is not self-directed action but cross directed action. And when we falter as partners, speaking out of turn, sleeping, and denying, may we hear the voice of Christ, as Peter did on the shore that morning eating fish with the Lord, to begin again to feed God's children.

CHAPTER SEVEN

The Zebedees

The story of the Zebedee brothers is one of two brothers challenging each other to work harder and dedicate more to a common cause. That cause of course was discipleship for Jesus Christ. The Zebedees were the first youth group and first young people to carry the mission and ministry beyond the security of the gathered people to a much greater audience. Their story is one of growth and development and differing paths that lead to a shared destination, lives devoted to following Christ.

The story of James and John draws my attention to the understanding that sometimes, being different causes conflict and friction. It's hard to find opposites that mold and meld together for shared success. Yet, it does happen. There are folks who could not be more unalike, yet their differences filled each other's gaps and filled the places of weakness with strength. That is rare but I have seen it with brothers, picking each other up, sharing their expertise to reach a perfect finished product. I remember two artists who had this knack. One drew the outline and structure and the other selected the colors and completed the product. It was amazing to watch them interact, knowing when to add and subtract within their reference of strength. These two artists worked together in the same way that James and John worked together for Christ.

The brothers John and James from the family of Zebedee were fishermen as well on the Sea of Galilee. "The frequent references to fish in the New Testament indicate that fish was an important part of the diet of the first century Galileans and Judeans. They ate fish, fresh and processed more than any other meat..."[57] The fishing industry held an important place within the lives of the local people. The Zebedees were no different. They were tied to the water in the same manner as a farmer was tied to the land. The difference noted here was that the Zebedees did have workers who assisted them and their father in the trade. Therefore their business may have been a bit larger than those run by Peter and Andrew. "Origin for example, identified James and John as sailors, 'When he (Celsus) calls them indiscriminately sailors, he probably means James and John, because they left their ship and their father Zebedee, and followed Jesus: for Peter and his brother Andrew, who employed a net to gain their necessary subsistence, must be classed not as sailors, but as the

---

[57] _John, the son of Zebedee: The Life of a Legend_, R. Allen Culpepper, University of South Carolina Press, Columbia, 1994, page 10.

scripture describes them, as fishermen."[58] Regardless of titles or work, James and John make their living as fishermen. There is no reference to ordinal position except that based on tradition, the ordering of the names reflects the birth order. Therefore, it may be read that James was the older and John was the younger of this sibling team.

The presentation of their titles and the fact that their father employed others outside the family to work on the boats including subcontracting to Peter and Andrew provides some indication that their financial position was higher than that of Peter and Andrew and that the Zebedee family were more connected, possibly more educated, and more available to travel with Jesus. In Matthew 20:20-21, we read:

Then the mother of the sons of Zebedee came to him with her sons, and kneeling before him, she asked a favor of him. And he said to her, "What do you want?" She said to him, "Declare that these two sons of mine will sit, one at your right hand and one at your left, in your kingdom."

The implication being that the Zebedees were younger than the rest of their fellow disciples because their mom was traveling with them and offering advice and an opinion to Jesus on the boy's behalf. We find the second clue from the Gospel Matthew 27:55-56:

Many women were also there, looking on from a distance; they had followed Jesus from Galilee and had provided for him. Among them were Mary Magdalene,

---

[58] *John, the son of Zebedee: The Life of a Legend*, R. Allen Culpepper, University of South Carolina Press, Columbia, 1994, page 14.

and Mary the mother of James and Joseph, and the mother of the sons of Zebedee.

This list of participants supports that the Zebedees had enough funds to send the sons as well as the mom along to discipleship with financial support for the itinerant preaching that was a part of the earthly ministry of Jesus.

Digging deeper into scripture and attempting to connect some scraps of evidence, the Gospel of John, reveals that a disciple was well connected enough to provide particular access to the inner sanctums of the Temple and the courtyard of the High Priest. In the Gospel of John 18:15-16, we find:

Simon Peter and another disciple followed Jesus. Since that disciple was known to the high priest, he went with Jesus into the courtyard of the high priest, but Peter was standing outside at the gate. So the other disciple, who was known to the high priest, went out, spoke to the woman who guarded the gate, and brought Peter in.

This points in the direction that a disciple was well connected, wealthy, and able to move freely in some of the circles of the people in power in Jerusalem. This is also supported in a text by Matthew Murray who writes, "There is also a statement by Polycrates the Bishop of Ephesus that John was a priest. The reason for this tradition is that the book of John makes reference to 'another disciple' who accompanied Peter into the courtyard of the high priest, because he was known to the high priest."[59]

---

[59] *The Sons of Zebedee*, Matthew Murray, Book Caps, Middletown DE, 2013, page 11.

The assessment of these facts points to the Zebedees as the members of the group who could very well be able to accomplish this and provide for financial assistance and lastly, be members of the Apostolic group.

The Zebedees are given the unusual nickname of the "sons of thunder" or "*boanerges*" which has remained one of the many linguistic mysteries of the Bible. "Interpretations of the Hebrew or Aramaic words that lie behind *Boanerges* do not explain why Jesus called the two by this name. Unfortunately, Mark gives no clues. Explanations have ranged from the suggestion that James and John spoke in loud voices to the conjecture that followers of John the Baptist, they witnessed the voice of heaven, spoke in thunder. Generally, however, interpreters have concluded that the name was given to the brothers because of the impetuosity of their natural characters."[60] The two young man for some unknown reason become the inner circle with Peter to observe the transfiguration as well as the closest partners at Gethsemane and then eventually John stays with Peter and brings him into the very courtyard of the high priest to witness the last moments of Jesus' life before the slow and painful experience at the hands of the Roman leaders and the cruel legionnaires' behavior. Culpepper asserts, "In Mark, the inner three serve as Jesus' closest companions, who witness the most secret, intimate events of Jesus' ministry."[61] From noisy youth

---

[60] *John, the son of Zebedee: The Life of a Legend*, R. Allen Culpepper, University of South Carolina Press, Columbia, 1994, page 39.

[61] *John, the son of Zebedee: The Life of a Legend*, R. Allen Culpepper, University of South Carolina Press, Columbia, 1994, page 37.

group members, to intimates of Christ, the brothers are a deep part of the ministry and movement that becomes the church. They splinter further, eventually putting John together with Peter as the Apostle referred to as the beloved of Jesus who is pictured with his head against the chest of the Lord at the Last Supper.

The brothers were filled with zeal and excitement for their work as fishermen, as priests, and as followers of Christ. James, the brother of John Zebedee was a passionate believer in Christ who demanded that his Lord be respected and adored and attention for himself. In the absence of this expectation he asked for consequences. It is important that James was more than a brother who called down fire on non-believers. He was a trusted and valued disciple of Jesus Christ.

This is a surprise as so little is known about him except his brief mission work and his martyrdom. Author John MacArthur writes, "This relative silence about James is ironic, because from a human perspective, he might have seemed the logical one to dominate the group. Between James and John, James was the eldest (That is doubtless why his name always appears first when those two names appear together). And between the two sets of brothers, the family of James and John seem to have been much more prominent than the family of Peter and Andrew."[62] Yet, James is not mentioned more often. However, the key to James is his relationship with Jesus.

---

[62] *Twelve Ordinary Men*, John MacArthur, Thomas Nelson, Nashville, 2002, Page 77.

MaCarthur continues, "Of course, James also figures prominently in the close inner circle of the three. James, Peter, and John were the only ones permitted with Him when He raised Jairus's daughter from the dead (Mark 5:37). The same group of three witnessed Jesus' glory on the Mount of Transfiguration (Matthew 17:1)...And he was included again with John and Peter when the Lord urged those three to pray with Him privately in Gethsemane (Mark 14:33)."[63] James is a trusted member of the inner circle who shows deference to Jesus and remains zealous in his beliefs about the Messiah.

The "passion" that James is credited with through John MacArthur's book is recognized by Jesus when he labels he and his brother, "Sons of Thunder." A key to understanding the name is explained by MacArthur as well, "Unlike Peter's name, which obviously was intended to help encourage Peter's character toward a rocklike steadfastness, 'Boanerges' seems to have been bestowed on the sons of Zebedee to chide them when they allowed their naturally feverish temperaments to get out of hand. Perhaps the Lord even used it for humorous effect while employing it as a gentle admonishment. What little we know about James underscores the fact that he had a fiery, vehement disposition."[64] It seems that Jesus was looking for a different kind of passion, a controlled passion that built up and did not tear down. In the same

_____

[63] _Twelve Ordinary Men_, John MacArthur, Thomas Nelson, Nashville, 2002, Page 78.

[64] _Twelve Ordinary Men_, Thomas Nelson, Nashville, 2002, John MacArthur, Pages 79-80.

way that Jesus rebuked Peter for wielding his sword so quickly on the night of his arrest, Jesus was guiding James in the direction of his more malleable brother.

John seemed to be more willing to follow the mentoring and leadership of Jesus and Peter. He was a bit more introspective, asking questions about who the Lord referred to while reclining at the last supper found in the Gospel of John 13:23-25 in the upper room. James struggled with the transition from passionate follower to compassionate follower. It happened, it just took much longer than his brother. His disposition is best captured by MacArthur when he writes about James, "Zeal without wisdom is dangerous. Zeal mixed with insensitivity is cruel. Whenever zeal disintegrates into uncontrolled passion it can be deadly. And James sometimes had a tendency to let his misguided zeal get the better of him...Two incidents in particular. The episode where James wanted to call down fire. The other is the time James and John enlisted their mother to help lobby for the highest seats in the kingdom."[65] James struggled with moving from passion to compassion, fury for God to forgiveness on behalf of the Lord. His love of God and enthusiasm was rich and eventually led to his martyrdom.

John was trained in the priestly work of his family tradition. While he certainly comes to Jesus as a rambunctious young man, he assuredly came to everything in that way. The meaningful process of holding the sacred

---

[65] *Twelve Ordinary Men,* John MacArthur, Thomas Nelson, Nashville, 2002, Pages 80-81.

with great respect and dignity is the transformation of John. The change in his entire demeanor is based on his experiences with Christ through the lens of priestly roots and foundations. We are reminded to hold the training of John in tension with the experience as a follower of Christ, "The fundamental task of the priesthood in Exodus, to bring Israel 'to continual remembrance before the Lord' (Exod 28:12, 29-30), stresses their intercessory role; this role is continued in Leviticus, but in view of the apostasy, their ministry focuses on the mediation of the word and deed of God to the people, especially the forgiveness…"[66] therefore we must consider John's vision as a bifocal between liturgical training and application of the experiencing the miraculous acts of Jesus Christ as the lens this brother witnesses the world. Therefore, John pens his Gospel with a foundation that produces the line, "And the word became flesh and lived among us…(John 1:14)" The journey of John is witnessing all the traditions of the Temple coming to fruition in this real-life religious experience with Jesus. The rituals of the priestly work had focus and intentions. The itinerant ministry with Jesus was not confined to theory and procedure but a living experience of God. The priestly life turns the attention of the whole community toward the words of Leviticus and holiness. "This does not mean that holiness is something to strive for: Israel's holiness is reality. The call to be holy (Lev. 19:) is a call to be true to the relationship in which the people already stand. Basically, this entails being faithful to

---

[66] *A Theological Introduction to the Old Testament*, Bruce Birch, Walter Brueggemann, Terence Fretheim and David Petersen, Abingdon Press, Nashville, 1999, page 133.

God in worship and in life. Israel's holiness is not simply an internal disposition, it is to be expressed externally in all aspects of life."[67] John throughout his time with Jesus witnesses all the prayers, rituals, actions, and beliefs come to fruition in Him. In being called to follow Christ, to leave behind the structure and expectations of his family business, in stepping away from the rigors and constraints of the priestly system, all that he mimicked and remembered was restored in this journey from Galilee to Jerusalem.

In the Temple, the priests were to maintain the holiness of the community by keeping the proper relationship on behalf of the Israel with God. It seemed that the priesthood had moved away from that understanding and replaced it with inflexibility and strictness to insure that contamination never occurred; the two entities, people and God, should never meet. Instead, the life with Jesus that John embraces is one that clarifies that the world could never contaminate God, the saving power of God is the detergent for a stained society. In the Gospel of Mark 9:38-39 we read,

John said to him, "Teacher, we saw someone casting out demons in your name, and we tried to stop him, because he was not following us." But Jesus said, "Do not stop him; for no one who does a deed of power in my name will be able soon afterward to speak evil of me.

***

---

[67] *A Theological Introduction to the Old Testament*, Bruce Birch, Walter Brueggemann, Terence Fretheim and David Petersen, Abingdon Press, Nashville, 1999, page 135.

John is taught by Jesus that the power of God is higher than the rules and limits of the institution. "In sum, the meaning of holiness is focus on distinctiveness and being set apart by virtue of the relationship with the indwelling God and in the service of a mission that is God's but set deeply within a world for the purpose of its sanctification."[68] John can see the Torah engaged in real life with real people that results in their healing and the restoration of humanity.

John is, as Joseph Campbell would express, on the "hero's journey," leaving the safety and confines of the theoretical, leaving the safety of the protected realm, to immerse himself in the true engagement of God in the dangerous world called life. When John accepts the invitation at the shoreline in Galilee he learns, "The adventure is always and everywhere a passage beyond the veil of the known into the unknown; the powers that watch at the boundary are dangerous; to deal with them is risky; yet for anyone with competence and courage the danger fades."[69] John's priestly service is one that prepares him to honor God and have a deep understanding and awareness of God's power and authority in the Jewish world. The Temple is a home for John that is very secure and molded by the ancient traditions. The opportunity to follow Jesus, to walk with a rabbi and learn his yoke is an

---

[68] *A Theological Introduction to the Old Testament*, Bruce Birch, Walter Brueggemann, Terence Fretheim and David Petersen, Abingdon Press, Nashville, 1999, page 136.

[69] *The Hero with a Thousand Faces*, Joseph Campbell, MJF Books, New York, 1949, page 82.

honor and privilege, however, the original context is within the first century structure and John would expect to be prepared for that task. The hero's journey he embarks on is clearly different where he comes to understand that in following Jesus, he is not following some ordinary rabbi but the very Son of God.

The journey that John takes with Jesus presses upon the very structure that he held dearly in his youth, casting him, "...into the crooked lanes of his own spiritual labyrinth... [which] when the senses are cleansed and humbled...this is the process of dissolving, transcending, or transmuting our infantile images of our personal past."[70] From witnessing healing, to feeding thousands, the transfiguration, and ultimately the empty tomb, John, who is following Christ, under the mentoring of Peter is drawn into this new stage that he is returning home unaware of the journey itself.

It is the early teaching and learning, the apprenticeship and the novitiate that forms the youth into the basic mold and model to go out into the world. Armed with parental love, reasonable resources, and the reassurance of teachers and guides, John the younger brother exudes a fresh confidence in the career, calling, or endeavor and begins on Day One prepared to conquer the world. This same spirit sends this "other brother" you and me to our first assignment, job, or classroom. The bell of the new school

---

[70] _The Hero with a Thousand Faces_, Joseph Campbell, MJF Books, New York, 1949, page 101.

year with untouched notebook and freshly pressed clothes never before worn beyond the confines of the family bubble. The pristine soul is the experience of John on the shoreline when Jesus calls him. This clean slate is the experience that we have, so sure and ready after our degree is earned, certification minted, title bestowed, and the literal or figurative hands are laid upon us to begin our work. We too, have voices of thunder, minds within formation and not wisdom, a saw with new teeth and not the grooves of many planks of wood cut. We too, are excited by the call to "join me," or "follow me" on the journey of "plying your trade" in our vocation. The opportunities are amazing to witness, to see the miracles and mysteries that the work has for each. However, with every destination comes a little more wear and tear. And just as the heteronym (tear) implies, for the roughing of the edges through the trial and tribulation, there is heartache and suffering in the tears of a person who grows wiser and has the luster of newness rubbed off and is replaced by the worn marks of maturity.

In the same way that John is lost in the crucifixion and Peter at the courtyard, we too lose a portion of our power and strength in those times when the sacrifice cuts the fibers that hold us together, sears the suffering into our skin, and leave us desolate before the death of our dreams and once firm understandings. And at the moment of sure surrender to the dark and evil, they are reborn in the light of the resurrection. This is the next to last step of the hero's journey, to return home but to see it with new eyes and a fresh sense of existence, the soul, the everlasting life in God. This is the next to last step back to geographic home. This clarifies that all that was true at the beginning is not only accurate, but much more beautiful, and holy than we were originally taught. John learns that the words of the Temple are not only true, but more powerful, more beautiful, and more saving than could ever be contained within the walls of any location. The love and mercy, healing and reconciliation is way more life giving and satisfying than anything he could study or imagine.

John returns to everyday life a changed man. He who was once a fisher and priest, returns an Apostle of Jesus Christ. As Campbell writes, "The first problem of the returning hero is to accept as real, after an experience of the soul satisfying vision of fulfillment, the passing joys and sorrows, banalities and noisy obscenities of life."[71] This life altering experience, the knowledge of knowing that we are really good and holy, chosen by God, assured in faith to act on behalf of the living God runs up against petty arguments, paying bills, gossip, and general unfocused efficiencies of life. It is astounding to measure a deep and holy experience of the transfiguration against arguing political viewpoints on the media, incessant junk email, and washing the dishes. In the midst of this, John holds this mystery of life, death, and resurrection. In the time and space of the present moment, he witnessed the alpha and omega, the arc of the entire reason for our lives.

---

[71] _The Hero with a Thousand Faces_, Joseph Campbell, MJF Books, New York, 1949, page 218.

John stands in the midst of a busy street and workplace with the true meaning of Jesus Christ in his very being and must decide the next step in the journey.

That comes to us in similar fashions. We have experienced in our lives the breathtaking beauty and love of the incarnation in deep relationships, in literature, in nature and search our minds to find the words to express our hearts. John is given the same opportunity that we are when we come to this crossroads. The decision is to hold this within and make it completely personal, separating from the world the shielding, the deep inner experience of the eternal or take the dangerous final step in the journey to express the beauty and majesty that we have been given as a gift of being close to God. The step that announces through words or actions or maybe both the gracious Good News of Christ. The freedom of love and the Kingdom of Heaven that operates under the economy of trust, compassion, and hope. This is direct conflict with an economy of distrust, greed, and pessimism. Many preachers, authors, and spiritual leaders describe this as a "thin place," a place where the one is feeling the breath of God on them, seeing the Eternal Kingdom, exposed from behind the weeds and wilderness of what we may think of as life and then decide to invite others into that new and wondrous place. This is the thin place that John resides. This is where the "other brother" distinguishes himself. John, the beloved disciple truly leans into the Christ experience and allows the danger and opportunity to unfold.

The Apostle John, whom we have traditionally credited with the fourth Gospel, the younger Zebedee and the beloved disciple, rested his life against Jesus, by resting his head against the breast of the Lord in John 13:23. The author Alan Culpepper writes, "The Beloved Disciple was reclining 'in the bosom' of Jesus which signals a privileged relationship."[72] John saw that the life that was in his heart came from Christ. He began in that moment, even though the trip would not be a straight and perfect approach, to remain closer and tethered to Christ even if he was viewed as someone who could only remain on the fringes of society, even exiled for his insistence on the Messiahship of Christ as a revolutionary position to the Roman authority and religious cultural rules. The hero's journey of John is the hero's journey that we are called to take in the name of God. The choice to lean into Christ and away from the accepted norms, the institutional expectations, and cultural systems is the way of this brother. It is clear, that he is not chasing or following ideas or causes or even the changing winds of newness, he is in the loving embrace of Christ.

The experience and expression of belovedness of Christ is there for us. The journey, the hero's journey, John's journey, and our journey are intertwined and are a shared path. Those things we learn about the goodness and love of God are true, and truer and more beautiful than is found in any written form but expressed in our belief, our faith, and ultimately our relationships with others. Our tether to God, our resting on the chest of Christ is the encouragement to

---

[72] *John, the son of Zebedee: The Life of a Legend,* R. Allen Culpepper, *University of South Carolina Press, Columbia, 1994, page 60.*

remain in that loving and secure place. When we view ourselves in the same way that John viewed himself we capture the authority of his and our "...unique role... portrayed in the Gospel as the one whom Jesus loved...had first grasped the reality of the resurrection and who had recognized the risen Lord...and knew that his testimony was true."[73] This is the power of this brother in each of us.

[73] _John, the son of Zebedee: The Life of a Legend_, R. Allen Culpepper, University of South Carolina Press, Columbia, 1994, page 85.

CHAPTER EIGHT

James The Brother Of Jesus

The story of James, the brother of Jesus is one of change and restoration. Originally, James finds himself siding with his sibling against Jesus, and not supporting the ministry of his brother. In the resurrection, James changes his mind, heart, and life to reorient himself to follow his brother, the Messiah, the Christ. The narrative of James is difficult if not impossible to duplicate, given the circumstances, however transcendence is the highest form of consciousness. James would be recognized as a pillar of the early faith, a uniter, and saint of the church.

There is no doubt that living in the shadow of a sibling is a challenge for every brother and sister. However the sibling of God incarnate is a level of shadow no one ever has or ever will again experience on earth. The fact that we have any knowledge of Jesus' brothers points to the results of their relationship more than the process of their relationship during his earthly ministry. I have known many people who lived in the shadow of a sibling. The shadow created by this brother seemed impossible to escape. The story of James simple has no parallel that I can think of for describing a relationship between two brothers. However the growth of John reflects the change of heart about our sibling, or a sense of distance between two brothers that is overcome by love and mission is something we can strive for and hold up as a place to grow spiritually and personally.

The story of Jesus found in the Gospels comes from the perspective of either disciples or Apostles. The narrative reflects the interactions with Jesus with his friends, with Apostles or disciples, with his parents and family members, religious leaders and community outcasts, Jews and God fearers, Roman soldiers and Roman prefects. The wide range of titles held and adjectives used to describe those who interacted with Jesus match their reaction to him. The reaction of these meetings leave people excited and angry, frustrated and embarrassed, threatened and, well, brought back from death. These interactions led to Jesus being described as rabbi and teacher, healer and troublemaker, miracle worker and eventually outlaw. Just as difficult as it was for strangers to understand Jesus, it seems that his family struggled as well.

Whether we consider the surrounding villagers of Galilee or the temple Priests, the positive attention or the negative attention, the shadow of Jesus' infamy or fame were hard for James to outrun. It was not as if Jesus was simply class president or captain of the sports team in high school, or big man on campus. The words used to describe him as Beloved Son of God in Matthew 3:17, Son of the Blessed in Mark 14:61 Savior in Luke 2:11, and Bread of Life in John 6:35, are just snippets from the Gospels. James would be aware of the names of Jesus and I am sure the footsteps would be much more difficult to follow in than any I can imagine.

The family of Jesus receives very little Biblical explanation which has led to a more significant amount of commentary and scholarly pursuit than would be anticipated. There are several schools of thought including the theory that Mary remained a virgin throughout her life and the siblings were from a previous marriage of Joseph or even cousins of Jesus. However, that speculation will not be addressed; instead this book is putting aside that argument, and considers the brother who receives the most observable attention in the text of the Bible which is James. We learn from John Painter, "While the earliest and most direct sources of our knowledge of James are the letters of Paul, these letters presuppose a knowledge of the fundamental relationship of James to Jesus."[74] We know that he is considered his brother and that he doesn't have the very best relationship when it comes to his mission and ministry as found in the Gospel of John 7:3-5 we read,

So his brothers said to him, "Leave here and go to Judea so that your disciples also may see the works

---

[74] *Just James,* John Painter, University of South Carolina Press, Columbia, 2004, page 11.

you are doing; for no one who wants to be widely known acts in secret. If you do these things, show yourself to the world." (For not even his brothers believed in him.)

The brothers were not impressed by the words and works of Jesus and made it clear that they were withholding support of him and invited him succeed elsewhere. Chilton and Nueser share that the interaction found in Mark 3:20-25 is a parallel negative experience upon Jesus' homecoming, "...the role of the family in this incident confirm that his known background makes acceptance of his new status difficult for the people of his hometown. What they know of his past overrides what they now find in him and leads to their rejection of this new Jesus."[75] This shadow cast on the ministry of Jesus from his family would be evident not only to him but to the closest of disciples. They would consider the family of Jesus as any group of followers as unsupportive and unaware of the teaching, preaching, and healing of Jesus.

As a result of these initial interactions, when James is engaged with the disciples, he is considered as "just James." In a time when the name James was so widely used, it was evident that whenever someone was going to use that name, an additional reference was required to clarify their place in the events, the interaction, and the relationship to Jesus.

---

[75] *The Brother of Jesus,* Bruce Chilton and Jacob Neuser, WJK Press, Louisville, 2001, page 25.

Examining the New Testament, a reader would see that a Zebedee was a James and the son of Alpheus was also a James, leaving three James in the same circuit. The multiple James' led to, at some conscious or unconscious level, the "just James" adverb. A reading of the early accounts would give the reader a sense that any sense of excitement or expectation would quickly dwindle, once the realization of the person as "just James" was identified.

Therefore, the decision of James to involve himself in the life of Jesus was a change in attitude and behavior toward Christ. By following Jesus, James steps out of the crowd of his family and moves into the realm of church leader and elder of Jerusalem as described in the Book of Acts. Simply put, "just James" becomes "James the Just." The ordinariness of James is replaced by the commitment that he demonstrates as a follower of Christ. "James emerges as the first leader of the Jerusalem church, the successor of his brother, Jesus. In his role he was effectively 'his brother's keeper.' From this perspective, tradition coming from James can be seen as a guide to the understanding of the mission and achievement of Jesus."[76] The brother James, who with his other siblings were turned away from Jesus, was able to reconcile himself to Christ and then become a counselor for the church. He who lived in schism with his brother brought together through his change those separated and unable to see

---

[76] _The Brother of Jesus,_ Bruce Chilton and Jacob Neuser, WJK Press, Louisville, 2001, page 24.

clearly their connection. The difference is how "just James" finds himself to be "James the Just." James, in fear of the detractors as well as the pressure to remain with the crowd experiences transformation that is transcendent. He is able to see the heart of others who once thought one way and could be opened to think, believe, and act in a different manner. James learns to recognize repentance and celebrate it as not only a constant command of his brother but a stepping stone to deeper union in the Trinity. James the Just, applies this gift as a leader of gathered people. "Whether or not James was an apostle, he presided at a famous apostolic council in Jerusalem that successfully healed a breach between the Jewish Christian community in Jerusalem and the factions missionizing to Gentiles in the Greek world"[77] His wisdom and objective authority was a part of his James the Just persona. James moved from the pack of dissenters to a trusted member of the newly created church.

In transition between the "justs" James experiences that the religious life that he hoped for may not have been what he planned, witnessed the unappealing struggle of Jesus and the heartache and suffering of the apostles. In the Lonely Man of God, we learn, "...religion at the outset is not, a refuge of grace and mercy for the despondent and desperate, an enchanted stream for crushed spirits, but a raging, clamorous torrent of man's consciousness with all its crises, pangs and torments. Turmoil and sacrifice, not

---

[77] _The Brother of Jesus,_ Hershel Shanks and Ben Witherington III, Harper Collins, San Francisco, 2003, page 26.

comfort and placidity, are, but divine edict, the hallmarks of authentic religious life."[78] James the "holy man" saw the religious life as one of quiet and prayer. The religious life, the work of a leader for God as one who calms the crowds and thrives under the administrative rule.

The spiritual and faithful life of Jesus was a call to true community, one that required a rabbi to hold sacred the suffering and pain of those in whom they held community. The Kingdom that Christ described was one that questioned authority because it established an equal footing for all people in the world because it was created by a loving and merciful Lord. James was adamant about his faith in Jesus the Christ and was martyred for his commitment.

James must learn anew the meaning of worshiping and serving a God of steadfast love. That required him to shift away from the crowd, away from the commonly held belief of many to, "go along and get along" to one of mutual life and livelihood. This was and remains counter to the culture of conquest and control. The actions of a person of justice and faith is a life of action and prayer that focuses, "...the covenantal nature of prayer community in which destinies are dovetailed, suffering or joy shared, and prayers merge into one petition on behalf of all."[79] The belief and subsequent action is a new learning, a new normal that James surrenders to, allows the light of this sunshine to warm his life and heart and turn him in the new direction of

---

[78] *The Lonely Man of Faith*, Joseph B. Soloveitchik, Three Leaves Press, New York, 1965, page xi.

[79] *The Lonely Man of Faith*, Joseph B. Soloveitchik, Three Leaves Press, New York, 1965, page 38.

leading the young movement. James is able to put aside the safe and comfortable to follow Christ and lead the church. Change is never easy and never comes without cost. However, change is possible when we allow the message to saturate all of us. As Soloveitchik writes, "The prophetic pilgrimage to God pursues a practical goal in whose realization the whole covenantal community shares."[80] James pursues a life with his brother that binds the new church and James realizes that the Good News is for everyone. He is challenged at all sides, most importantly, he is challenged within. The spiritual struggle of James is exactly what Soloveitchik described, as holding the conquering and covenantal parts of our hearts together in one single being. "The man of faith, in his continuous movement between the pole of natural majesty and that of covenantal humility, is prevented from totally immersing in the immediate covenantal awareness of the redeeming presence, knowability and involvement of God in the community of man."[81] This is an amazing balance of participation and separation, action and prayer, seeing God in all aspects of life and Christ in every face of humanity. That is a steep hill to walk, and deals us the hand for how the word "just" will be laid at our feet. This is the place of James, the brother of Jesus. Our task is to remain open and do the same.

---

[80] *The Lonely Man of Faith,* Joseph B. Soloveitchik, Three Leaves Press, New York, 1965, page 59.

[81] *The Lonely Man of Faith,* Joseph B. Soloveitchik, Three Leaves Press, New York, 1965, page 76.

CONCLUSION

We each start out on a path. To some, the path may seem obvious for what it is or why we are on it. For others, it may take a lifetime to find that moment of clarity that pulls a variety of threads into a woven tapestry. My Other Brother is no different. As one of three sons, we referred to the brother not in the room as "your other brother." The pronouncement was at best, made in jest sometimes, at other times sarcasm, as well as spoken in a manner that was hurtful and humorous, and it has remained a part of the family lexicon. In some way, I have found that the stories of the Bible resulted in some kind of triumphant ending, some kind of valuable "take away" that changes our life. Sometimes, it feels like life does not give us that happy ending or satisfactory conclusion. The strands don't always come together to bind up our family story. It is my hope that this book will provide clarity and space for pause and reflection about those dangling strands. In the absence of immediate answers, I hope that it encourages each of us to keep the search alive. I pray that this book is a help, for all of us, you and I, your brothers and my brothers. I feel as if there is something desperately important in it all. The relationship, even if it holds only a lesson that cannot be shared for some reason, doesn't become lost on our searching heart. This is a book for your journey and mine, your experience as well as your friends' and brothers' experiences. The difference between everyday life and spiritual consciousness is not as simple as life in the dark and life in the light. Enlightenment, universal entanglement, or spiritual fullness are not best described as flipping on a switch and living a life where we always know God and know ourselves. Instead, spiritual consciousness is more aptly described by Abraham Heschel as lightning in the night sky. Heschel describes the moments of connectedness with God as noticing the flashes of lightning in the evening sky. The more in tune a person becomes the more flashes they notice. Heschel recognizes that some never notice the flashes at all and live in total darkness while others, rare as these holy people are, enjoy far more flashes that allow the observer not only the chance to see the light but also to experience the landscape in an illuminated state. "The flashes are important, however what they reveal is also important to our understanding of the landscape or the world."[82] I hope this book can be a flash in the dark, a moment of bright light and visible direction in a sometimes dark and unseeable journey. I hope together we can shine some light on this thing called brotherhood.

---

[82] *God in Search of Man*. Heschel, Abraham. *Farrar, Strauss, and Giroux. 1983. pg. 140.*

The siblings described here had the spiritual gift of seeing far more flashes than their brothers and sisters. The landscapes in which their lives played out appeared differently to them and hence they fulfilled their lives set apart from others including the most intimate people in their lives, their brothers.

I am reminded of this quote as it pertains to our understanding of the Bible and our lives, "Every text of scripture is there not simply to take up space, but because it is given by the spirit of God and contains some theological concern which prompted it to be taken, by God's providence, into the canon."[83] Our lives are written as canon to our journey with God. No less valuable than the saints written of in the past and no less inspired than any other sibling, our stories matter. We, as children of God, have been given a life with many twists and turns that seem unclear. I hope this text will provide just a little more vision for this and the many curves we find ahead. I hold each brother in prayer. May these words expand the horizon, spotlight the hope, and give you energy to climb the next mountain. Let's remember that the journey is better together.

---

[83] _Our Father Abraham_, Marvin R. Wilson, William B. Eerdmans Publishing and Center for Judaic-Christian Studies, 1989, p. 115.

ACKNOWLEDGMENTS

To God be the glory...

Words cannot describe the thanks I have for everyone who gave of themselves to help with this project, family, and friends, brothers and sisters alike who helped make this happen. Your editing, thoughts, ideas, and expressions of support made this happen. To the One who Reigns, thank you for your inspiration and the energy to cross the finish line.

Made in the USA
Middletown, DE
28 February 2019